Mindful Teens & Pre-Teens: A Practical Guide With Examples, Meditations, Tips To Help Manage Anxiety, Depression, ADHD; Provide Pain Relief, Boost Immunity & Improve Sleep Quality

Dana Mayho Taylor

Table Of Contents

Introduction 1

Chapter 1: What Is Meditation? 5

Tips for Success Through Meditation 9

Benefits of Meditation 14

Meditation & Yoga, The Perfect Compliment 15

The First Limb 17

The Second Limb 19

The Third Limb 21

The Fourth Limb 21

The Fifth Limb 22

The Sixth Limb 23

The Seventh Limb 23

The Eighth Limb 23

Breath Control Options for Yoga 25

Chapter 2: How To Make It Easier To Meditate 29

Getting Started With Meditation 31

There's an App for That! 33

Guided Meditations Are the Best Thing Since Sliced Bread 37

Guided Mindfulness Meditation 37

Stress Reduction 38

Relaxation 39

Exercises & Cases 42

Chapter 3: Surviving Anxiety With Meditation 46

Stress.. 49

Acute Stress 49

Chronic Stress 50

Anxiety 51

   Activity 1.. 54

   Activity 2.. 55

   Activity 3.. 56

Anxiety Disorders 57

Agoraphobia (ag-uh-ruh-foe-be-uh) 57

Generalized Anxiety Disorder (GAD) 58

Panic Disorder 59

Separation Anxiety Disorder 60

Obsessive Compulsive Disorder (OCD) 61

Social Anxiety Disorder... 63

Specific Phobia.. 64

Substance-Induce Anxiety Disorder........................... 65

Post Traumatic Stress Disorder (PTSD)..................... 67

Exercise: Emotional Awareness 70

Managing Stress, Anxiety, and Fear........................72

Nip Negativity 73

Break Out Your Journal! 75

Examples of Journaling Ideas 76

Don't Forget About Doodling 77

Identifying What Causes Your Stress 79

Activities..83

Be Self-Compassionate 85

Self-Compassion Worksheets 87

Chapter 4: Coping With Depression Using Meditation 88

Adjustment Disorder...90

Dysthymia 90

Bipolar Disorder..91

Major Depression 91

It Only Takes 10 Minutes 95

Mindful Steps To Help Relieve Depression.........................97

What Are Your Depression Triggers? 98

Do You Run on Autopilot?....................................100

Account for Emotional Avoidance..........................101

Exercises 102

Breath Awareness Meditation or Mindful Breathing .103

Using Positive Affirmations 104

Change Your Mindset 106

Building Your Focus Through Aromatics 108

The Benefits of Being Active 109

A Closer Look at Mindfulness 112

Five Short Chapters 116

Exercises & Case Studies 118

Chapter 5: ADHD 122

Inattentive Type 123

Hyperactive Impulse Type 124

Combined Type 124

Exercise and Case Study 133

Remember To Be Silly 137

Meditation 138

Yoga for ADHD 142

Chapter 6: Meditation for Guided Healing 148

Does meditation help? If so, how? 151

Great, but why is meditation effective? 152

Relief of Chronic Pain 153

A Boost for Immunity 164

Chapter 7: Achieving Better Sleep .. 178

Are you an early bird or a night owl? 184

Meditation for Sleep Disorders 184

Insomnia 185

Having Problems With Your Sleep? 190

Periodic Limb Movement Disorder (PLMD) & Restless Leg Syndrome (RLS) 190

Obstructive Sleep Apnea 193

Idiopathic Hypersomnia 197

Narcolepsy 202

Night Terrors 207

Sleepwalking 209

Exercises for Mindful Sleep 210

One-Minute Meditation 210

Insomnia Can Be a Real Struggle 211

Surrender Meditation 213

Schedule Yourself a Time to Worry 214

Chapter 8: Meditations – Writing Your Own 219

The General Structure of a Guided Meditation 222

Guided Meditation Example #1 224

Guided Meditation Example #2 227

Conclusion 229

A Guide Activities, Exercises, Tips and Case Studies 233

Activities 233

Exercises 234

Tips 235

Case Studies 236

About the Author: 238

One Last Thing 240

References 241

Image References 245

A Letter to the Parents

I wanted to reach out to the parents who have picked up my book in order to help both themselves and their teenagers through some potentially troubling times and ease your mind regarding the benefits of mindfulness and meditation. If you are unfamiliar with the art of mindful meditation, the insights within this book will help both you and your children learn about the practice of meditation and the many positive benefits it brings to the practitioner. It will also clear up for your family any misunderstandings you may have regarding mindfulness and the empowerment it can give you on the journey through life. Let me assure you that the practice of mindfulness and meditation offers a world of benefits for the practitioner.

You and your teen may find it beneficial to practice these methods together, learning ways to open your hearts and providing understanding about empathy, managing stress, and bringing balance to life. Through mindfulness, you have the ability to open up communications and become aware of your thoughts and feelings. I believe that mindfulness can be especially beneficial in the development of communications between parent and child.

Whether you have had a long day at work or your teens have experienced a long day of classes and peer pressure, the ability to come home, disconnect from those experiences, and remembering to just breathe can help regulate and balance emotions and behaviors.

I have taken time to assemble strategies of positivity using meditation so your family can experience the transformative power of mindful living. There is never a better time to begin your journey than now.

Dana Mayho Taylor

Introduction

Being a teen isn't the easiest part of life. Teens struggle to balance homework, home life, perhaps a part-time job, and a busy social life. Their mind and body are busy with so many changes that it's tough to keep up. When you add in the factors that teens don't ever seem to get enough quality sleep, struggle with peer pressure, seek social acceptance, and face bullying, stress, and depression, it's enough to fill ten plates, let alone one. Since each teen is an individual, the way that their best friend handles stress may be very different from their own.

Besides all the factors that teens may juggle in their daily lives, they can also struggle with their self-esteem and are constantly worried about something someone may say about them. When a teen is worried about fitting in and avoiding trouble, it can be hard to know who to trust with confidential information. During this period in a teen's life they can experience big social changes, emotional changes, and relationship changes. All of these stressors are preparing a teen to become an adult.

Learning to face fears is never easy, nor is it something that needs to be figured out all at once. Check in with your emotions throughout the day and acknowledge anytime you feel fearful. Should you be experiencing some fear, sit down and breathe. By practicing how too focus on your breathing, you can push through the terror you may be experiencing and you may find that the fear remains, but how you react to it is different. Help from others is available and from them one can develop their own sense of patience and kindness for oneself and others.

Your ability to deal with negative feelings is a lot stronger than you normally give yourself credit for. When running away from strong feelings, you instill in them a power they don't actually have. Perhaps you suffer from an innate fear that your feelings will be too much to handle, so you shy away from them. Maybe you have a feeling of unworthiness to experience anything positive. None of that however, is true.

When you learn to ride a horse, you do not jump a grand prix course your first time in the saddle, because learning to ride is a process and you take lessons to become a better rider. A good teacher will start you off learning your balance at the walk, trot, and canter. Step by step, you will master these skills and if you want to move forward into jumping, there are many stages and miles to be ridden before you would ever get to those big jumps. Learning how to meditate and express your feelings can be thought of in much the same fashion.

According to the National Institute of Mental Health (2020), an adolescent brain reaches its full size during the preteen and teen years. It's a time when the adolescent brain is changing, readying a person to become an adult. And it does not happen at the same rate for all of us. Girls peak at about eleven years of age and boys reach the full-size brain around fourteen. Even after the brain is done growing, it still continues to mature and typically does not finish developing until somewhere around the age of twenty. The front part of the brain is called the prefrontal cortex and is one of the last regions of the brain to mature. All of an individual's skills like planning, prioritizing, and control impulses are controlled by this area. It's no wonder why teens sometimes display risky behavior during this time because their skill set is still in development.

A brain during the teen years is when the mind is most pliable, meaning that during these formative years is the easiest time to adapt to changes, rise to higher academia, and respond to creative activities that can help the brain learn and mature. It is also during adolescence when mental issues begin to appear. While a brain is busy changing, its environment can put physical, social, and emotional pressures on a subject that can emerge as issues such as stress, anxiety, depression, and bipolar disorder because of vulnerability. Because of the psychological process of paying attention to the present moment, mindfulness can help teens work through their stresses.

The next important teenage factor is sleep. Teens need a lot of it, much more so than any child or adult. The teenage body produces a sleep hormone known as melatonin. The levels of this hormone are higher late at night and drop late in the morning. Teens should really be sleeping around nine to ten hours each night, but because of hormone levels, they are often unable to go to sleep at a reasonable time and they are forced to get up early for school.

The good news is that the teenage brain is resilient. Within this book we have included information on meditation, mindfulness, and yoga and how to use them to combat the effects of stress, anxiety, ADHD, depression, and sleep disorders.

During the teenage years, there is a lot that happens to an individual. It is during this time that teens are moving away from being a child and being treated more like an adult. This is a time when they are trying to figure out what they want to do, decide upon hobbies that interest them, and stand at the beginning of defining themselves and what makes them unique.

Meditation, mindfulness, and yoga can help you discipline your mind, calmly focus on your future and find your happy place.

Chapter 1: What Is Meditation?

"It's a lifelong gift, something you can call on at any time." – Sir Paul McCartney, singer/songwriter

Meditation has been around for thousands of years. According to Giovanni (2018), the oldest documented piece of evidence that demonstrated the practice of meditation was depicted in wall art that dated somewhere between 5,000 and 3,500 BCE. The practice of meditation has been represented in Ancient Egypt and China in the beliefs of Sikhism, Jainism, Hinduism, Judaism, and the most well-known of all, Buddhism.

Meditation may have had its beginnings in many religions, but it is a practice that can be followed independently of any religious or spiritual beliefs. People who practice mindfulness come from both non-religious and religious backgrounds.

If you have any hesitations about participating in meditation, we recommend you consult with your parents, guardian, mentor, or other professionals you trust.

Meditation lights the way for the transformation of your mind, heightening your awareness and making you more conscious of the world around you. During meditation, you learn to focus on your breathing and pay attention only to the present without any concern to the past or future. Meditation is all about the new discovery of you.

The thought of starting something new, like the practice of meditation, probably adds a bit of worry to your mind, but meditation is actually quite simple. It involves the application of regulated breathing, focus, and allowing your mind to wander, but bringing it back to your original object of concentration.

You can choose to utilize a mantra, but it isn't required. Meditation is a steady cycle of being focused, acknowledging distraction, and gently reminding your mind where you were.

Mindfulness meditation is comprised of 3 basic steps:

- Paying attention to an anchor, for example a mantra
- Allowing distractions to occur, because they are inevitable
- Letting go of your distraction and returning to your anchor

The above sequence can be repeated as often as necessary during each session of meditation.

Even though meditation is often practiced by different religions, it may also be performed free from any religious ties. Cultures from all over the world have practiced and benefited from the study of meditation.

Your soul can be fed through the art of meditation, whether you write in your journal, go for a walk, read things that interest you, draw, write poetry, listen to music, or just sit and snuggle with your dog. Any of these things can bring you happiness and draw you in to the present moment.

Although meditation is a universal name for practicing a relaxed state of being, it is all about self-discovery. There will always be a new takeaway. Whether it's a new approach, new thoughts, or new methods, you will never learn it all. With so many jewels in the meditation crown, we are all but beginners exploring the facets.

Meditation is the cure for scattered thoughts. If we train our minds to focus on one thing at a time, this increases our ability to concentrate. According to Harvard researcher Sara Lazar (1994), various studies have confirmed that meditation changes brain function for the better. Those brains are less likely to become distracted than those that don't meditate.

Though there are different techniques that center around the art of meditation, they all share a common goal, to attain peace.

There are some different ways to meditate:

- **Guided meditation.** A guided meditation can be spoken or recorded and builds its message around relaxing places or events. Typically the guided meditation incorporates music and the spoken word. The practitioner could be at home listening to a recording or in class with a trainer.

- **Mantra meditation.** The use of a repeated mantra can help release the mind and support those experiencing difficulties in concentration. Your mantra may be silent or spoken.
- **Mindfulness meditation.** This type of meditation encourages you to focus on being aware of what you are experiencing in the moment. Using mindfulness, you are discouraged to interpret or pass any judgments. When you engage in mindfulness meditation, you are also involved in breathing methods, guided imagery, and more.
- **Qigong.** (pronounced chee-gong) Qigong originated as an ancient Chinese exercise that includes healing techniques. The practice of this meditation combines physical movement, breathing exercises, and relaxation. There are many forms of Qigong practiced worldwide. Qigong can have a healing effect on your bodily systems and provide strengthening to calm mental and emotional states.
- **Tai chi.** Also originating in China, tai chi is a gentle form of martial arts known to increase health benefits and meditation. These exercises were developed to have one graceful movement flow into the next so that you can easily incorporate deep breathing. According to Harvard Medical School (2019), there exists growing evidence that this mind-body connected practice has value in the treatment of many health issues. Most of the movements of tai chi are circular in motion and should never be forced. Tai chi can be utilized by anyone, from mobile children, those recovering from surgery, or an individual

confined to a wheelchair. You can learn from a class or utilize recorded sessions.

- **Transcendental Meditation®.** Transcendental Meditation was created in India in the mid-1950s by Maharishi Mahesh Yogi. This simple and completely natural technique involves sitting in a comfortable manner with your eyes closed for about twenty minutes each day and using a silent mantra. This practice allows you to achieve quieter levels of thought. While the TM technique is easy to learn, it is advised that you study with a certified teacher.
- **Yoga.** Yoga is not merely exercise. Yoga is a meditation. Through yoga meditation, you learn to quiet a busy mind. Yoga meditation provides the ability to focus your thoughts, leading to a true presence of being in the moment. During your series of chosen postures, you incorporate breathing exercises that combine both mind and body.

Tips for Success Through Meditation

Above we have discussed what meditation is, its origins, and the different types of meditation, but how exactly does one meditate successfully?

Most pursuits in life are best experienced by starting at the very beginning, and meditation is no different. It is frustrating to jump into anything midway and become overscheduled and overwhelmed. By making this choice, anyone can easily become unmotivated with the discipline.

Start by picking out a spot where you can practice free from any distractions. Now for the tough part—you should turn off your phone and any other electronic distractions you have running in the background. You can, of course, play music, but you should choose something calm and with no vocalization. Your choice must provide you with a quiet and calming atmosphere. You may also find something suitable on a sound machine. For example, picking a calming thunderstorm or white noise may prove beneficial. You may find that you prefer to have total silence. Background sound is a personal choice and totally up to the individual.

Dedicating a special spot that you use each and every time will help you to establish a needed routine. It doesn't matter if you meditate for five minutes or twenty, you should try and schedule it for roughly the same time every day. Just like a sleep schedule is important to maintain, so is a meditation routine. It's important that you find the time of day that works best for you. Many people find that morning is the best time to meditate, but if you have early morning class, that may not be possible. Perhaps you would benefit from a brief session after school to assist you with your homework or just before bedtime if you have sleeplessness issues.

Even if you can take just a few minutes each morning, it can help set you up for the rest of the day. A little meditation in the morning can bring about a calmness that lasts your entire day so that you feel ready to face whatever may present itself throughout your day. What's important is that you find the time of day that not only works best for your busy schedule but provides you with the most benefit.

A Note From the Author:

You should be able to practice mindfulness and meditation anywhere, at any time. Should you have an early morning class, try to incorporate meditation into your morning routine, while getting dressed, for instance. Focus on your breath and what you are doing at the moment.

- *"I am breathing in."*
- *"I am breathing out."*
- *"I am putting my left sock on."*
- *"I am putting my right sock on."*
- *"I am tying my left shoe."*
- *"I am tying my right shoe."*
- *"I am putting on my favorite green sweater."*
- *"I am putting on my jeans."*
- *"I am putting my phone in my pocket."*
- *"I am breathing in."*
- *"I am breathing out."*

Whenever you begin to feel distracted or start worrying about an upcoming test or class, take time to notice your thoughts. Remind yourself that your brain has wandered off and that class is still two hours away. Gently, bring your mind back to the present.

- *"I am breathing in."*
- *"I am breathing out."*
- *"I am walking down the hall to gym class."*
- *"I am still breathing in."*
- *"I am still breathing out."*

That's it! Anytime you feel that you could use a small time to settle your mind, simply apply your focus to what is happening in the present.

After a session of meditation during the morning hours, you should take a few moments for reflection before racing off for a busy day at school or wherever you need to go next. When you do this, you destroy the calm that you have worked so hard to achieve.

When you are getting started, make sure that you set time limits. Shorter sessions help new practitioners become more confident. You can always build upon your five initial minutes of meditative practice, and before you know it, you will feel like an expert.

One of the most important things you must keep in mind is to be comfortable. It doesn't matter if you sit cross-legged on the floor, are seated comfortably on the couch, or lounge outside in a tire swing, because it is all about what works best for you. A typical position for a beginner is to sit upright in a reasonably cozy chair. Make sure that you will remain comfy for the duration of your meditation time. If sitting isn't working for you, there are other options such as lying down or taking a walk. With more practice in meditation, you will gain confidence and may even want to take your sessions outside for a walk with Spot.

Nature provides its own meditative experience where you can watch birds, take in nature, or just listen to the sounds produced by the rustling wind. Any experienced horseman can tell you that there is no better way to lose an entire afternoon than on the back of a horse. There is much to enjoy while spontaneously picking trails to explore in a forest preserve. So, enjoy your walk or ride and take spur-of-the-moment directional choices so you are not focusing on a given destination.

Most teens can really be into their wardrobes and are dying to ask that burning question, What do I wear? There are no set rules to what one should wear, but it is recommended that an individual be dressed comfortably so relaxation is maintained. Avoid anything too tight or binding.

There can be misunderstanding about meditation. Some believe that the purpose of meditation is to clear your mind, but that's not true. Meditation is the practice of focus, and when your thoughts inevitably drift, you don't obsess about why your thoughts strayed, you merely bring them back to where you were. Open mind meditation is to fully accept what is going on in the moment without reacting to it in any way.

Mindfulness Activity

Get out a paper and pen and let's try a mindfulness activity!

- Picture a person who has had a positive influence on your life. Write down what it is about that person that you admire most. How would you like to be more like that person?
- You are all grown up, What are you doing with your life? What kinds of friends do you have? Describe them.
- Write a full description of a time you were truly inspired. What inspired you and why?
- List ten things that you love to do. It doesn't matter if it's camping, fishing, boating, reading, or painting.
- If you had a chance to study anything for a day with no interruptions, what would it be?
- If you could spend an afternoon talking with any person throughout history, who would it be? Why would you choose them? What kind of questions would you ask

them?
- Everyone has something that they are good at, perhaps several! What are you good at?

Benefits of Meditation

Meditation and mindfulness have been practiced over centuries for good reason. They restore mind, body, and soul while boosting your defenses against disease. Meditation fosters wellness within the body and spirit.

Meditation can:

- Help you combat stress
- Ease headaches
- Diminish the symptoms of anxiety and depression
- Improve self-awareness
- Increase your sense of compassion toward yourself and others
- Improve immunity
- Develop better focus
- Deal with insomnia, thereby improving your sleep
- Lower high blood pressure

Teens are able to center their attention and remain calm because of meditation's effects on anxiety. Daily use of meditation makes one more mindful of their actions, so teens will develop an inner wisdom, which will enable them to make better choices.

Meditation & Yoga, The Perfect Compliment

Meditation and yoga go together like green eggs and ham. When you meditate, you delve into your heart and work to develop a calmer, well-balanced mind. Yoga was designed to support the practice of meditation while calming your nervous system and cleansing your body.

Sometimes when you practice one form without the other you find something missing from your routine. For example, if you come home from a great yoga class, you may still feel a little uneasy, as if you were losing your inner stability. People who practice yoga may become obsessed with the fitness aspect and forget that meditation is the key component to help them ground their minds. Because meditation and yoga together strengthen the connection between mind and body, it is possible to become a bit preoccupied with the body and forget that your mind also needs to be along for the ride.

Of course you can practice one without the other, but when used together and consistently, they provide the practitioner with better health benefits. The following list provides a few examples of meditation and yoga working together.

- Improved muscle suppleness. It's important to note that many classes or jobs today have you sitting a lot at your desk. The daily repetition can put strain on your body, in particular on your neck and shoulders because of being hunched over a computer for long periods of time. This position can also cause your brain to become overtired. Yoga helps increase your flexibility and lengthen your muscles. Meditation can help improve your focus, especially when you find your thoughts drifting away. There are many athletes who incorporate both practices into their workout schedules to keep their minds and bodies operating at top performance.

- Stress management. Meditation is a successful group of methods to reduce conditions which can lead to stress, anxiety, panic disorders, and chronic pain. Yoga can likewise decrease stress responders in your body and can reduce your chance of stress-related conditions.
- Enhancing your health. When you add the combination of meditation and yoga into your daily routine, you can only improve the quality of your life. Who knows, you could add years to your life expectancy!
- Improve your diet. Because yoga can improve your fitness and body awareness, it quite naturally raises your self-esteem. When you have a higher level of self-esteem, you develop a desire to take better care of your body and mind, thus you will find yourself making better dietary choices and opting for an orange instead of a Twinkie. Meditation and yoga together will help you improve your behaviors and your overall self.

Yoga and meditation are body-mind practices, but what are their differences? Since we have already talked about meditation earlier in this chapter, let's focus on yoga.

The practice of yoga helps you gain awareness over your body and mind while using a variety of poses or postures to increase strength and flexibility. The principal purpose is to make one strong, healthy, and peaceful.

How old is yoga? We don't have an exact date, but we do know that it started out in India over five thousand years ago.

Some people become confused thinking that yoga is a religion, because it emanated from a religious country. Yoga is not a religion and never infers that you should honor any religious figure. The only thing that yoga does ask is that you create a strong bond with yourself.

Yoga is a Sanskrit word meaning to join or unite. This has been interpreted to mean that you want to join your mind, body, and soul with the surrounding world. Yoga has been defined in eight different ways and is described using the concept of limbs. The eight limbs of yoga are based on a comparison to branches found on a tree. There is no one single branch of yoga that is more important than another. All branches of yoga unite in one ending: peace. In order to achieve peace, we must practice them all.

The First Limb

In yoga, the first limb is known as Yamas. Yamas is a Sanskrit word that defines the five rules you need in order to be good to other people, the world, and yourself.

The first Yama is Ahimsa, meaning kindness. When you first begin to practice yoga, you are taught to be kind to all people, including people who are not nice. The first Yama in yoga believes that if you are nice to everyone, you are less likely to become upset or angered. Achieving this makes you a happier person.

The second Yama is Satya, meaning truthfulness. We are taught through yoga to always tell the truth in a kind way. By being honest, you do not create stress and remain a happy person.

The third Yama is Asteya, which translates as non-stealing. Yoga tells us that we are not to take anything that is not ours. Unfortunately, our world is full of people who steal, but yoga encourages us to be the change. Asteya doesn't categorize theft, so it doesn't matter if you swiped a pen or a car; stealing is stealing. When you take from others, you lose the goodness within.

The fourth Yama is Brahmacarya, which instills in you the importance of your body. Yoga discusses how important it is that you not use physical touch for anything other than the connection to your spiritual self. While on the search for yourself, realize that it takes time to discover who you really are. Through Brahmacarya, you learn to respect your mind and body.

The fifth Yama is Aparigraha, which translates as non-greediness. Yoga instructs us that it is important to share what you have with others. In order to become a selfless person, you take only what you need and dedicate the rest to others. When you perform being selfless, you set an example for others to be givers as well. Today, you may refer to this as paying it forward. The whole idea of helping others is to convey peace and harmony into the world.

The Second Limb

In yoga, the second limb is called the Niyamas. While the Yamas (above) talk about being a good person to the universe, the Niyamas try to communicate to you that you must also be a good person to yourself.

The first Niyamas is Sauca, which refers to cleanliness. This expresses that it is imperative you keep your inner and outer self clean. Besides washing your body and brushing your teeth, you should be wearing clean clothes and keeping your possessions organized. In order to keep your inner self clean, yoga stresses eating healthy foods and exercising. We should also practice happy thoughts.

The second Niyame is Santosa, which through translation means being content. When you look around you, there are many things you should be grateful for in your life. For example, you can be grateful for the roof over your head, heat if you live in a cold place, or if you have something to eat. Contentment teaches us to be ok, because life often throws us a curveball and not everything appears as rainbows and unicorns. Yoga teaches us that the secret of being content all the time is to be grateful for what you have.

For example, the next time you are angry with your parents or think they are being unfair, take a moment to realize that you have parents, and be grateful for that. There are many out there who would consider themselves lucky to have a parent. Be happy, for when a person is content all the time, that happiness becomes connected to your mind and body.

The third Niyamas is Tapas, or self-discipline. When you discipline your actions, you do what you say you are going to do. Your mind and body need to be at optimum strength, so wasting your time on social media for hours might not be the best use of your time. We are not saying to ignore your friends on Instagram completely, but perhaps only a short time each day is appropriate and then spend the rest of your time reading or writing something that inspires you.

The fourth Niyama is Svahhyay, a practice in self-study. In order to make you a better person, you need to know yourself. If you are aware that something is going to stress you out, then remove it from your life and replace it with something else. If that something is immovable from your life, practice your contentment and gratitude until it has passed.

The fifth and final Niyama is Isvara-pranidhana. This Niyama talks about the act of taking care of yourself by surrendering. Throughout the course of your life, there will be a multitude of things that you cannot control. This fifth Niyama helps you to understand that this can and will happen, there is a purpose behind it, and everything will eventually be ok.

The Third Limb

The Asanas are what the third limb is composed of. Asanas are Sanskrit for postures, and this is the part of yoga that is the most practiced in the United States. Leave it to the Americans to skip ahead to the fun stuff! The third limb teaches us the importance of moving and stretching our bodies. The Asanas each address different things that focus on making your body stronger. Depending upon the position, they can help detox your body, encourage strength to your organs, or prevent future sickness.

Being nimble and physically strong is important, but you should never lose sight of the fact that you need to be a good person at heart. Yoga is not restricted to doing the splits on a mat, it is used to make you feel good all of the time.

The Fourth Limb

The fourth limb is named Pranayama, which means breathing. Nothing really stresses the importance of proper breathing like yoga. The majority of people do not truly experience how to take long breaths. Without them, their bodies cannot reach the strength or the calm that they are capable of.

The following branches of yoga turn their focus to meditation. Meditation can be difficult for some people to get the hang of at first, but yoga can teach you some methods to get your mind calm and focused. The ability to focus is easy if you are doing something fun and have an interest in it, but how is your ability to focus when the task doesn't give you as much pleasure? With the help of meditation, we can slow all those thoughts whirling around in our heads and live life to the fullest.

The Fifth Limb

In yoga, the fifth limb is called Pratyahara, which focuses on meditation to help calm your mind and control your senses. This instructs you to stay focused and remove things that might distract you. Let's say that you are studying in your room, but your sister has decided to make some brownies in the kitchen. With such a great smell permeating the air, you are not going to want to focus on studying. To practice Pratyahara, you could physically move outside or go to a friend's house; or the library to study, but yoga teaches us how we can shift our attention so we are able to shut out what is going on around us. Being able to shift your focus will take some advanced control, but with dedicated practice in Pratyahara you will become more focused and less distracted.

The Sixth Limb

The sixth limb in yoga is called Dharana, which means concentration. Our world has become so full of digital distractions that focus and concentration are becoming lost arts. Right now, just try your hardest to concentrate and focus your attention on what is going on right in front of you. Can you do it? Don't worry if you cannot right now, because this can take some practice to perfect. Just keep trying to pay attention to what is happening around you and don't get distracted.

The Seventh Limb

In yoga, the seventh limb is Dhyana, and this translates to observation and reflection. It's actually pretty straightforward that if you can observe your actions and reflect as you are performing that action, then you are practicing Dhyana.

The Eighth Limb

The eighth and final limb is called Samadhi and it is a place in your mind where you can feel completely at peace. This happens when you are not distracted by anything and can truly claim to

23

be in the present moment and thinking of nothing. To reach Samadhi is to experience bliss. The practice of all the limbs will get you to this point.

So how do you do yoga?

The limbs of yoga that we have just gone through explain that yoga can be done anywhere because not all yoga is done on a mat. You experience yoga through being kind, honest, and respectful as well as by stretching and meditating.

Life can be a rollercoaster of emotions. You can be happy, sad, angry, nervous, or scared. One day may be filled with laughter and the next with tears, but yoga and meditation teaches you how to take care of yourself though mind and body so that you can have more joyful days than sad ones.

Breath Control Options for Yoga

"Inhale the future, and exhale the past." – Unknown

It makes no difference if you are stressed, happy, sad, or tired, you never stop breathing. Subconsciously, we inhale and exhale all day, every day. We never hear people comment about breathing since most people just don't give it much thought. It is rather amazing when you think about it, because we can't survive without breathing. It is the first and last thing we do in our life and yet we ignore it. Yoga teaches us to breathe consciously.

Taking conscious breaths helps us develop our diaphragm muscles and develop the ability to take deeper breaths. By following this practice, we can call upon these fuller breaths at any time, even when we are not meditating or doing yoga.

If you feel mad, taking deep breaths will instantly ease your anger. This can be beneficial in keeping you from saying or doing something you might regret later. When we become irritated, the first thing we do is forget to breathe. As this happens, our heart responds by speeding up and our adrenaline kicks into overdrive. If you can remember your deep breathing exercises, you will find your heart rate returning to normal and you will feel calm.

What happens when you become frightened? You probably stop breathing. Watch any scary movie out there and you will probably see a lot of screaming, running, and gasping for air, because when we are frightened, we forget to breathe. Being frightened is more difficult than dealing with anger, since when you are panicked, you don't always think straight. Focusing on your breathing will help you call upon it even when the situation is dire.

Deep breathing is a powerful management tool when dealing with our daily stresses. The great thing about deep breathing is that you can do it anywhere and no one even notices that you are doing it. You don't have to fear relaxing; you can and should be able to let your guard down. Begin slowly and you will be able to build your skills over the course of several weeks.

- Breath awareness. Through observation, we pay attention to each individual breath. During breath awareness, we take notice of the expansion of our lungs and the sensations we experience in our nose and throat. We can also manipulate our inhalation and exhalation by trying to deepen them.
- Nostril breathing. We can choose to breathe through a right or left nostril depending upon what we are trying to achieve. If you breathe in through the right nostril, you are looking for a heating quality and if you breathe in through the left nostril, you are looking for a cooling quality. Nostril breathing can be performed in a variety of patterns: Anuloma Ujjayi, Viloma Ujjayi, Pratiloma Ujjayi, Suryabhedana, Chandrabhedana, and Nadi Shodhana.

- Control of the breath flow. We can manipulate our respiratory musculature to achieve directionality to our flow of breath. As an example, we can choose to either breath first from our diaphragm or our chest.
- Vocal breathing. Often referred to as Bhramari, vocal breathing creates both sound and vibration. Sound can energize our system and we can manipulate both the volume and pitch to become either more soothing or stimulating.
- Krama breath. We can break our breath into segments of up to 2-3 parts during inhalation or exhalation. This particular method is often overlooked, but can have a very noticeable energetic effect for the practitioner.
- Breathing ratios. With this practice, we can gradually lengthen parts of our breath. Broken down into four parts, we have inhalation, retention, exhalation, and suspension.
- Valved breathing. To add a vibrating quality to our breath, we can choose to breathe through the valve that we form in our throat or mouth. Valved breathing also helps to lengthen breath.
- Kriyas breathing. Because this utilizes rapid breath, this is considered more of a cleansing practice. This is performed by repeating a lower abdominal contraction in a seated, cross-legged position.

Let's focus on breathing!

- Make yourself comfortable.
- Focus on your breathing.
- Bring your right hand up over your right lung and your left hand over your left lung.

- Inhale deeply through your nose.
- Notice the air that travels all the way down your throat and into your chest. Focus on this as your hands and your lungs rise up.
- Picture your lungs as two balloons. As you do this, try to fill them up so they are holding as much air as they can.
- When you are unable to take in any more air, exhale, and picture the balloons deflating. Notice where the air chooses to depart.
- Add counting to your breaths and now breathe in two counts, and out two counts.
- Continue to repeat these steps and try your hardest to focus on how you breathe and how many counts you can achieve.

Chapter 2: How To Make It Easier To Meditate

"Meditation is my passion. I think a lot of people are so used to being stressed, they don't realize they're stressed. And I was one of those people." – Ricky Williams, NFL Miami Dolphins

Break the cycle. If you make a change in your meditation behavior, you will begin to feel better. You may find it hard to believe, but it's true that your mindset can change how you think. We know that your stresses aren't dismissed simply because of the way you think, but it can be helpful for changing your outlook.

Everyone faces challenges. Sometimes we allow them to limit our beliefs, causing negative habits. If you want to succeed, you have to continue to practice. For example, if you want to play the piano, you need to work at it every day in order to become more skilled. You put in the same amount of training each day and it should not depend on whether you have a lesson the next day or not. You feel great and have accomplished your scales and have begun to learn your first real piece of music that isn't tied to a rubber duck or rowing a boat.

You are just getting ready to sit down and practice your piece when a friend calls and distracts you from the day's rehearsal. The following day, your best friend wants to go shopping for her prom dress and invites you to come along and give her your opinion. You concede, because, really, how often does prom come up? Okay, now you have missed two days worth of practice. After coming home from school, you and your mother get into an argument because you aren't practicing your piano lessons that you begged for.

In just a short time, your plans have been derailed and your goal of playing the piano is in serious jeopardy because you start believing that you have no will power and cannot stick to a routine. Perhaps you are thinking that it was too hard to fit it in anyway and you should give up on your dream.

Small thoughts like these invade our mindset and talk us out of our direction in the world. We start empowered, but let distractions get in the way of accomplishment. It's completely true that meditation can change your mindset. We have already mentioned that meditation can help you become more focused and train your mindset, but it can also aid you in envisioning new possibilities.

Once you realize that there is no such thing as perfection—only persistence—will you begin to show yourself more kindness. The small act of practicing a two-minute meditation each day will bring you a new outlook and a new way of thinking.

The core principles of meditation are very simple. If you are thinking that there is some hard work and effort that you will need to put into forming a meditation habit, then you would be correct. Every new habit takes effort. The good news is that I am right here to help you with steps and tips to make your journey easier.

- Know that some days you will fail. Everyone does, sometimes even a string of failures. Accept that it happens, don't punish yourself for it, but simply move on.

- Willpower is overrated. You have to learn to give yourself a break because sometimes it isn't easy to will yourself to follow the same energy zapping schedule every day, it can be exhausting. As above, don't punish yourself if you give in.

- Start small and be consistent. It is better to have a two minute meditation every day over the course of a month than a weekly 10 or 20 minute session. If you are able to start small and build, you won't even realize that you are spending that time. You will thank yourself in the long run.

- Don't fall apart because you skipped a day or two. Let's face it, stuff happens. You might not be able to meditate for a day or two, but you can set your schedule for the third day and begin anew. You can commit to change and keep going.

So what's your first step? One of the most difficult obstacles you will have to overcome is simply getting started and staying with it.

Getting Started With Meditation

Remember to be kind to yourself when you are beginning this journey. **Meditation is not focused on how perfect you can be, so don't worry about perfection**. There is no need to panic if you miss a day here and there, because there will be other days when you meditate.

Stop waiting for the perfect time to meditate. It works best if you pick a time and make a schedule that you follow. Stop saying that it's not quiet enough or you are too distracted. There are some pretty good excuses out there, but none of them are good enough to dissuade you from sitting down and getting started. So, stop telling yourself that you aren't in the right frame of mind, because meditation is all about getting you to the right place.

You can tie meditation to something you are already doing. We all have our favorite routines that differ from person to person, but whether it's enjoying that cup of coffee, or taking Spot out for his morning constitutional, you can meditate even if it's just 5 minutes each day.

Pick a space to meditate. Put familiar things in this area to make it more likely you will follow through on meditation. You might choose a special cushion or pillow, or something personal like a candle, singing bowl, or a crystal that has special meaning to you.

When you begin to meditate, you want to keep things simple while you are in your learning stages. Please find below an excellent place to start.

- Lie down, or sit comfortably. Now close your eyes.
- Make no effort to control your breath. Just breathe normally.
- Focus on your breath and how your body moves with each inhalation and exhalation. Describe how your body moves as you breathe. Take notice of your chest,

shoulders, rib cage, and belly area. Without trying to force your breathing, just pay attention to the rise and fall as you breathe. If your mind begins to wander, that's okay, just return your focus to your breath.

- When you are first beginning, this practice can last 2-3 minutes, but as your confidence increases, you can try it for longer times.

These tools can give you an idea of what kinds of meditation styles are out there and what they are like. Many of them will offer you advice on how to structure your meditation.

There's an App for That!

Another way to help you begin the practice of meditation is by utilizing a meditation app or a guided app. While we are in no way affiliated with any app or game on the market, some of you may find the list below worthy of checking out. Some apps allow you to schedule reminders so you don't forget to take time away from your stresses and get some needed relaxation through your meditation. Whether you are a beginner, someone who meditates daily with ease, or someone highly skilled in the art of meditation but struggles to find the time–there is an app just for you! We took the liberty of checking out many of the apps on the market and recommend both of these because they center around students and possible challenges they may be facing, such as struggles at school, social events, and home life. Both of these apps are free to the user, so with parental permission, download them and take them for a spin.

UCLA Mindful. If you want the ability to practice your mindful meditation exercises anywhere and anytime, then this could be a fantastic solution for you. The UCLA Mindful Awareness Research Center encourages the use of mindfulness to help you manage anything stress or anxiety-related. UCLA offers you a timer to use for your meditation sessions and videos with important tips for you to get started. They even have a wellness meditation choice that is offered for anyone afflicted with overwhelming health conditions. This app offers you, the user, in-depth information on how to get started in mindfulness and also offers the following:

- The option of both English and Spanish language
- Informative videos
- Support for encouraging the development of positive emotions
- Nurturing improvement for your well-being and overall physical health
- High-quality meditations
- Completely free to the user

Smiling Mind. This app offers choices to students who are struggling with a solution for a problem that is getting out of hand. There isn't anyone out there who doesn't have five minutes to spare, and during that time, this app will assist in comforting a user who needs to calm down and take some needed deep breaths. Teens need help learning how to manage their everyday stresses, and Smiling Mind is right there with them offering solutions that benefit the user just before class or a big exam. There is no right or wrong time to meditate, so if teens need nighttime meditations to help them get a good night's rest, then Smiling Mind is there to help you every step of the way. Designed in Australia, Smiling Mind is a not-for-profit app providing additional activities and session podcasts that give you, the user, specifics of each lesson, meditation, or activity. It doesn't matter if someone is a beginner or a seasoned meditation practioner, Smiling Mind has designed their service to work for any age group or level of experience. Smiling Mind will help an individual track their progress as they move forward through the various lesson plans, meditations, and exercises.

For a teen who is into gaming, the Playne app may provide just the outlet they need. This app has been chosen for our readers because of the beautiful graphics it provides and because it promotes a completely peaceful atmosphere. Players begin by following along step-by-step in the pursuit of meditation knowledge. Playne involves its users by making them a participant in a story which they can influence by meditation. The user has the ability to build their own personalized habitat to perform meditation routines within the game. Playne will keep track of how often and how long one meditates within their realm. Being a pioneer, Playne has developed a different and unique approach to the introduction and practice of meditation. The program was designed for anyone who has little to no experience in the art of meditation. While performing meditations within an individualized gaming world, the player can watch their own personal world blossom and transform. Playne can be found at: https://www.playne.co–a meditation game found on Steam. Always consult with parents or a doctor before use.

Guided Meditations Are the Best Thing Since Sliced Bread

For the beginner, a guided meditation is a great way to get started and get your feet wet. A guided meditation can be done in a group setting or alone. These meditations are written by and recorded/spoken by another. The appeal is that you don't have to work on any visualization or put any thought into the meditation storyline. You can find a large variety of guided meditations out there on apps, podcasts, videos on YouTube, or CDs.

While on the hunt for the perfect guided meditation, there are three popular forms of guided meditation for you to pick from:

Guided Mindfulness Meditation

As a concept, mindfulness may be simple, but you may find it more difficult than you thought. We all have our minds trained to behave a certain way and now, all of a sudden, you want to change everything and make your mind do something completely different from your norm. The teen mind is all over the map when it comes to thoughts. A teen girl can be walking down the hallway to her next class and she wonders if she has time for a quick stop at her locker, she notices that a classmate has a different hairstyle and she wonders how that might look on her, there's a cute boy over there she has never seen before, and ideally, she wonders if she has time to do her nails tonight. But the practice of mindfulness is all about staying put. One can still experience those daydreams and random thoughts, but instead of following them, an individual must encourage their mind to focus on the present and support that meditation with deep breathing.

After some practice at guided meditation, you will find that you can now practice sitting and meditating at your own pace.

Stress Reduction

With stress reaching epidemic levels in teens, mindfulness can help your mind, which can be overrun with stressful thoughts, to remain calm and focused. According to the Mindworks team (2020), the mindfulness practice has been known to relieve stress. They gently introduce you to the mindful way to practice relieving your stress. Besides guided meditations for stress relief, there are also guided meditations that target other areas like relaxation and sleep.

If you are experiencing difficulty falling asleep or staying asleep, a guided sleep meditation may enable you to let go of your anxieties and get the best night's sleep that you have had in a very long time.

Relaxation

What could be more comforting than trying something new and being guided by someone else? Through these meditations, you can balance your emotions while listening to calming sounds, descriptions of peaceful environments, and receiving an invitation to experience a land free of anxieties and restlessness.

When your guided relaxation session is complete, you should return to the world slowly. If you jump back into the hectic pace of your life, you can set everything back that you have just accomplished. Allow yourself to rejoin the world slowly while lingering in the present moment. Open your eyes and slowly return to your daily life. You will find your energy enhanced, and your mind will be clear.

Case Study: Terri

"Growing up in my home was very confusing. My parents had different religious beliefs and it seemed like they were always fighting about it. I was confused because I ended up not knowing which way to turn and they were each pressuring me to pick a religion. I found it difficult, because I really didn't know enough about either one to commit to a way of belief. Then came the divorce. Bouncing back and forth between the two of them was like being a large piece of taffy caught in a machine and I became depressed for reasons that I couldn't really understand.

"I tried talking to my friends, but they really didn't seem to understand my situation. I struggled through high school and made it to college, but as soon as I settled in, I found that I was once again depressed. For some reason, it was more intense than when I attended high school. I awoke one morning and found myself paralyzed with fear because I realized I had no direction and nothing brought me happiness. I had reached bottom, a point where I was seriously considering taking my own life. I felt all alone.

"My roommate and I really didn't know each other well, but she sensed that something was wrong. When I opened my mouth, everything rushed out, and to my surprise she didn't seem overwhelmed. She invited me to listen to her guided meditation audio files and I started to practice the guided meditations with her. I had never given meditation much thought, because I thought it was religious and I didn't need a third choice causing more havoc for me. That was the day that changed my life. I found out that meditation is for everyone and there were no rules governing how I chose to practice. I have meditated every day since then, and I no longer feel torn and can make good decisions."

Guided Meditation Example

Try your hand at your own guided meditation with a recording or a friend! You can each take turns reading this to each other or make up one of your own.

Go to your comfortable place and lie or sit down. This exercise will take approximately fifteen minutes, so make sure you won't be disturbed. Make sure that you are in comfortable clothes. You can dim lights, light a candle, put on some soothing music, or place some crystals in your space. Now allow your body to sink into whatever surface is directly beneath you.

Take three deep breaths from your diaphragm, and with each inhalation, imagine breathing in only relaxing energy. Now with your exhalation, imagine breathing out any worries and stress you may be keeping inside. Focus on your awareness within your body, and if your attention should wander (because it will), just take notice of where it has visited, and then gently bring it back to now.

While taking your next breath, point your toes outward until you can feel a stretch. As you hold this for the duration of a few breaths, notice any sensations you may experience and then return to normal position.

Next, curl your feet toward you and feel this new stretch. Do you notice any tension in your ankles or in your calves? Hold this position for a few breaths also before returning to your original position. Be aware of any changes.

During the next several minutes, slowly experiment with your main muscle groups by tensing and holding them. After releasing each one, notice what that feels like, both emotionally and physically.

Take special notice of the areas of your lower back, stomach, and upper back areas because these are typically the regions in the body where we carry the largest amounts of stress.

You may ball up and then stretch out your hands and fingers before moving on to your biceps and triceps. Again, if your mind wanders, just notice that and breathe in relaxing energy, and breathe out your stress. Focus, and bring your body back to the present.

The next area is also a place where you hold stress; this is your neck and shoulders area. Take special notice of any sensations or emotions as you tighten and release in these areas.

Move on to your face muscles and try to be aware of how your face feels from the inside. You can manipulate your face by furrowing your brow, squeezing your eyes shut, scowling, or smiling. Take notice of how this feels and then relax your face.

The last area where you can hold onto stress is your jaw and it can be displayed by grinding your teeth or clenching your jaw. Tense your jaw muscles tightly for a few breaths and then release. When you finish this exercise, you should feel the release and relaxation course through your body. After you begin your regular day, if you feel tensions returning to certain areas, just tense them and then release, thereby deflecting the storage of stress.

Exercises & Cases

Exercise 1

When you begin the process of healing, you must learn to tolerate all of your feelings, even the difficult ones. You will find that feelings don't last forever; they tend to come and go like waves that crest off the ocean. Some are weak, some are tsunami-strong, but none of them are everlasting.

While you practice getting in touch with your feelings, keep paper and pen nearby and imagine yourself to be a dolphin, using your power as necessary to ride out the waves of your feelings.

Now, allow your thoughts and feelings to wander through depths of the vast ocean.

Your thoughts will come and go like the waves. They are steady and peaceful. Some waves/feelings may appear to be stronger. There is nothing wrong with that, it's normal. Remind yourself that you do not need to be preoccupied with each wave. You are a dolphin.

You must continue to swim. Assign each wave with a negative feeling such as anger, sadness, or worry and then let it go.

Continue with your swim for up to 5 minutes. At the end of this exercise, take several deep breaths and then write down your thoughts. Did you find this exercise easy or difficult? How did you feel—safe or unsafe?

Exercise 2

Teens need to express themselves with self-esteem-building affirmations. You have life experiences and need to recognize your strengths. One way to remind yourself of your best qualities is through affirmations. They are good for your self-esteem and used by many top athletes and successful people around the world. Let's begin with a few examples of your talents:

- I follow my dreams.
- I am creative.
- I consider myself to be kind.
- I have value.

- I learn something new every day.
- I make great choices.
- I am learning who I am.
- I am a fast learner.
- I work hard.
- I am a good friend.
- I am kind and caring.

You may have been through a lot lately. Based upon your lifetime of experiences, how would you like to see the world change? When you believe in your own strengths, you are able to endure the difficulties that life can throw at you.

What kinds of goals do you want to achieve in the future? College? Write down what you want your life to look like in the future. Do you have a purpose in mind that is something bigger than just yourself?

Take time to review your affirmations and goals. Make a plan for how you will achieve them months or even years from right now. Let your mind wander and write your plans down.

Put your creativity to work and take that list you wrote down featuring your talents and goals and hang it up somewhere that you will see every day. Dreaming about your future is a great way to plan and follow through on the life that you want. With goals, support, planning, and practice, you can achieve almost anything.

Case study: Ashley

"I felt destined to never know happiness. I was seven and an only child. My mother had passed away from cancer, leaving just my father and me, so our relationship grew even closer since we were all each other had. But my father traveled a lot for work and I was left with a trusted caregiver.

"The years passed and I was gathering a few supplies for junior college. I will always remember that day. It was the day that I received a phone call from state troopers about an accident my father had been in while out of town. A drunk driver had hit my father's car head-on and killed him. I think it was safe to say that I was devastated. I was able to stay in my home and begin school, but my life was filled with sadness and anxiety.

"My anxiety kept me afraid when my friends would travel out of town. I was always worried that something might happen to them and I had nightmares while they were gone. I began to wonder if there was something within me that brought bad luck and death to those around me. First my mom and then my dad. I cringed every time I thought about them and worried about who would be next.

"Thank goodness for my friends. I had a great group that I had hung out with for years and I eventually told them about my thoughts. They assured me that I had nothing to do with the death of my parents and told me what a kind person they all thought I was.

"My friends made sure that I ate regularly and would check in to make sure I was getting proper sleep. A few of them would come over every day for the longest time to help me with some basic yoga and guided meditation tapes that they had been using. Because of their support, I was able to deal with my losses and realize that I was a good person who deserved to be happy and was not a grim reaper."

Chapter 3: Surviving Anxiety With Meditation

"What I think meditation is doing is erasing that line between challenge and stress. You can take on increasingly more and more challenges without it becoming stressful." – Dr. Fred Travid, brain researcher

Being a teen isn't easy, but if you are a teen who is dealing with stress and anxiety, that is going to make your life much harder. Everyone has stress. No matter where you live or what you do with your spare time, stress is right there alongside you. You can experience a mild amount of stress if you are perhaps running late for an appointment and the restaurant is taking forever to get your order done.

"I always experienced difficulties for a few nights before a big test. My mind just wouldn't settle down after a night of studying. I always worry about what the essay questions will be pertaining to or if I even studied the right materials. Even after I finally do fall asleep, I wake up constantly after nightmares of being late for class, not knowing any of the answers on the test, or turning in a blank essay. My best friend helped me to understand that I was feeling anxiety. She taught me a few deep breathing exercises that I could do right before bedtime and again right before the test. It really helped me get my anxiety under control before it got out of hand. Now I use this technique every day to help me better control anxiety attacks." – Chantell, 16

Stress and anxiety are actually two different things, but both are associated with depression (discussed in the next chapter). Stress is predominantly a feeling of emotional or physical threat. Your body reacts to threats or pressures by increasing your heart rate or producing sweaty palms. Depending upon the magnitude of the stress you are experiencing, you may find you have trouble concentrating.

Stress

When stress lasts a considerable amount of time, it may start to harm your health, but you may be surprised to learn that in short bursts, stress can actually be a positive thing. If stress enables you to avoid something dangerous, or when you are under pressure to get that paper in on time, it can help you get moving.

There are two main types of stress.

Acute Stress

This is a short-lived stress that is in and out of your life pretty quickly. For example, a skunk races out in front of your car and you are forced to slam on your brakes. Acute stress helps you to diffuse some potentially dangerous situations. This is also what happens when you begin a new job, try to decide on just the right outfit to wear to homecoming, or start a new grade level. Everyone experiences acute stress from time to time.

Similar to a prey animal, our brains respond to acute stress in the fight-or-flight response. Our brains send out neurotransmitters that cause adrenaline to produce changes within the body during our response.

Your heart rate and blood pressure increase, rocketing blood to your major muscle groups. This explains why your feet or fingers may feel cold and clammy. During your response, your body and mind make drastic changes in your immune system, your digestive system, and your mind. You probably weren't aware that your mind was capable of changing all these systems as quickly as a herd of antelope changes direction because of a cheetah. Once the threat is over the mind kicks into the relaxation response and all systems return to normal.

Chronic Stress

If you experience a stress that lasts for a long period of time, then this is considered chronic stress. If you are experiencing trouble at home or problems at school that never seem to end, you may have become so accustomed to the incidents so that you stop realizing that it isn't normal. Chronic stress can so on for weeks, months, or even years. This is the kind of stress that can affect your health. And, if you already have an existing health condition, stress can obviously make it worse.

Chronic stress weakens the immune system, which is what we all use to fight diseases and protect us from infections. Chronic stress is also known to worsen afflictions such as allergies, asthma, and autoimmune disorders.

Chronic stress affects every system within your body, but people are not built to handle the long-term effects of chronic stress. Attacking both physical and psychological systems, chronic stress can take a toll on your ability to function in a routine manner.

Individuals deal with stresses in their own way, but stress can manifest in some very frightening ways, such as substance abuse.

Signs of too much stress:

- Headaches
- Lack of focus
- Lack of energy
- Aches and pains
- Experiencing forgetfulness
- Shortness of breath
- Tight or aching muscles
- Developing sleep disorders
- Upset stomach, diarrhea, or constipation
- Weight loss or gain
- Substance abuse
- Feeling out of control
- Feeling helpless
- Constantly worried

Anxiety

Ever feel those butterflies fluttering around in your stomach as soon as the teacher calls upon you to stand up and read your paper aloud to the class? That is a normal anxiety response to an everyday situation and we all experience them. In cases such as these, anxiety may work in your favor, helping you to focus on your efforts and put your best effort forward.

You may begin to experience difficulty performing daily activities and experience feelings of being panicked and out of control. If you are avoiding people or places in order to circumvent these feelings, you may have escalated to an anxiety disorder.

If you are suffering from an anxiety disorder, you are not alone. According to Jason Porterfield (2014), the National Institute of Mental Health (NIMH) reports that eight percent of teens have an anxiety disorder, but only eighteen percent of those afflicted teens seek help.

Why are so many teens suffering from severe anxiety? No one right now is certain, but they do attribute the rising numbers to high expectations, a world that becomes more frightening every day, and being constantly connected to social media. Teens should be vigilant and aware of the symptoms they can experience with anxiety.

You can suffer from more than one type of anxiety disorder, and it could be caused from a medical condition that should never be ignored. Speak up and talk to your parents, because this is important stuff!

Anxiety takes on those flight-or-fight responses and ups the ante by adding emotional and behavioral elements. If you are suffering from anxiety, are you ever concerned about a future occurrence that most likely will never happen? Do you worry that every hurdle will end with the worst possible outcome? If you do, then you are probably filled with feelings of hopelessness, apprehension, and nervousness.

Common symptoms of anxiety are:

- Feeling nervous or tense
- Always feeling like there is a looming sense of impending danger, panic, or doom
- Experiencing an increased heart rate
- Rapid breathing, or hyperventilation
- Sweating
- Feeling weak
- Feeling exhausted
- Having trouble concentrating
- Having difficulties separating your mind from a current concern
- Trembling
- Experiencing trouble sleeping
- Having gastrointestinal problems
- Inability to control your worry
- Complete avoidance of things that trigger anxiety
- If you are feeling depressed and experience problems with substance abuse
- If you feel fearful and have difficulty controlling your anxiety

An anxious person can't help being irrational because they are dominated by being over analytical, obsessed, and worried. What a person may fail to realize is that anxiety is not an enemy to fight, but rather an important heralder of messages. You can struggle with control only to find that it exacerbates the problem instead of providing you with a solution. Your journey is to discover what your anxiety is, and then follow methods that break down each step so that you succeed by way of acceptance, mindfulness, and valued actions.

You cannot outrun anxiety; instead, you need to stop running and let your thoughts and feelings be there. Sure, they are going to bring challenges, but you will find that they are important and will bring a greater understanding and mindfulness to your life.

Activity 1

Create a simple spreadsheet with columns that represent the following: thoughts, feelings, behavior, and sensation. When you are experiencing something that makes you anxious—for example, the feelings of butterflies fluttering in your stomach—which column would you put a checkmark in? Write down things that make you anxious, then put a checkmark in the appropriate column. Some examples might be those found below, but you will have others more specific to you.

- Your heart races
- You have difficulty breathing before you have to give a presentation at school
- You missed out on something important and it makes you angry
- You experience everyday worry
- You feel light-headed and don't feel a connection to anything
- You turn down a friend's request to attend a party because you think everyone will feel that you are boring

Activity 2

Make notes every time you feel anxious, and try to use detail when describing them.

- Describe any feelings you experienced.
- What thoughts ran through your mind?
- Were there any physical sensations?
- What did you do to counteract these feelings?

Use the following as a guideline the next time you feel anxiety creeping in.

- Situation:
- Thoughts:
- Feelings:
- Physical Sensations:
- Behavior:

With these two exercises, you have been able to put a face on your anxiety. Your next step is trying to overcome your feelings of being stressed out or nervous. Remember to be kind to yourself and not become mad for experiencing these feelings in the first place.

Activity 3

We are all guilty of using control strategies in order to reduce our anxiety, and occasionally that's acceptable, but there can be some long-term consequences if you continually attempt to control your anxiety. No matter how you might try to trick yourself into believing you have everything under control, anxiety is still going to be there running in the background like a virus that invades your computer.

As above, consider actions you have used to control your anxiety and make a few columns to describe what you did to control the anxiety, the benefits you received, and whether there were any consequences.

What happened later? Was the anxiety gone for good, or did it come back? How would you describe the intensity? Was it less, the same, or more?

Try comparing your mind to your cell phone picture gallery. Recall a moment from earlier in the day and try to remember as many details about them as possible. This might be difficult, but delete that photo from your mind just as you would delete a photo on your phone that was out of focus or one of those photos of the floor that one might take by accident.

Were you able to delete the photo from your mind? If so, ask yourself what was the subject matter of the photo you deleted? If you are able to answer this question, then it isn't really gone, is it? This is a bit of a trick, but it should have driven the point home that it is nearly impossible to delete our memories, thoughts, and photos.

No one will ever be truly free of anxiety, but you can be determined to not let it control you. When faced with anxiety, it is important that you should practice being kind to yourself since anxiety is inherently hardwired into us all. Remember that everyone is subject to the same struggles that you face, so you are in good company. Your anxiety can be controlled and lessened through your mindfulness exercises.

Anxiety Disorders

We know that anxiety is an everyday, normal part of life, but what happens when you begin to feel worried and have a growing fear concerning everyday life? The symptoms of anxiety disorders take on the resemblance of ordinary anxiety, but turn excessive in nature. There are several types of anxiety disorder.

Agoraphobia (ag-uh-ruh-foe-be-uh)

This anxiety disorder causes you to fear places or situations because the result is panic. This disorder makes you feel helpless, trapped, and embarrassed. Some sufferers of agoraphobia never even leave their homes and have a panic attack just stepping outside of their front door.

A teen that experiences panic attacks along with agoraphobia will characteristically avoid places, circumstances, and situations that they believe will increase their likelihood of experiencing an episode. They fear having a panic attack in a place that they would find difficult to extract themselves from.

A few examples of teen agoraphobia might include staying away from large crowds, malls, or sporting events. Some have even shown a fear of transportation, so they begin to fear being in a car, bus, or airplane. Their fears will continue to build until the only place they feel safe is within their own homes.

Generalized Anxiety Disorder (GAD)

When you suffer from GAD, you are constantly worried about events or activities. This is not limited to special events, but can revolve around ordinary, everyday routines. The worry expressed over an event is typically out of proportion to actual circumstances, but those afflicted with GAD have an enormous amount of difficulty controlling how they feel. If your anxiety level becomes impossible to control, it will take a toll on your schoolwork and social life.

If you suffer from GAD, you probably suffer from headaches, fatigue, and muscle tension. What causes GAD is not known, but it does tend to run in families and often emerges during the teen years.

Panic Disorder

It's normal to feel a little anxiety and become nervous or jumpy before a big event, but someone who suffers from panic disorder has panic attacks, which surface in seconds, reaching a peak in mere minutes. They can feel fear or absolute terror and have a meltdown referred to as a "panic attack." You may experience symptoms during a panic attack like a racing or pounding heart, chest pain, or shortness of breath. Some sufferers have even complained of feeling paralyzed, being smothered, or feeling completely out of control. The length of a panic attack is usually around ten minutes. What's surprising about this disorder is that there is often no initial reason for the attack to take place.

After panic attacks start, they continue like a domino effect for the people experiencing them. Teens begin to worry about the next attack, and the next, and so on. Their mind tells them to avoid places where they have had an attack before, so if you had a panic attack on an escalator in a department store, you will continue to avoid both escalators and department stores.

If the attacks continue to disrupt your life, you may not want to go out in public at all. What starts as panic disorder can develop into full-blown agoraphobia.

During the late teen years is a common time for panic attacks to surface and is often associated with other conditions such as substance abuse and depression.

Separation Anxiety Disorder

Although separation anxiety is usually associated with younger children, it can carry over into the teenage years. It can cause a teen to have major problems with leaving home or going to school. Some separation symptoms may include:

- Distress about being away from home
- Worry about something bad happening while away from home, such as becoming lost or kidnapped
- Excessive concern about losing a parent to an illness or a disaster of some sort
- Refusing to be away from home
- Panic about being the only one at home without a parent or other family member in the house
- An unwillingness to sleep away from home without a parent or family member
- Experiencing nightmares about separation
- Frequent complaints of stomach aches or headaches
- Fear of being without a parent or caregiver

While all the causes aren't known for separation anxiety disorder, certainly genetics can be a factor, as well as environment and life stress that resulted in being separated from a parent or loved one.

Obsessive Compulsive Disorder (OCD)

Practically everyone prefers a sense of order around them, where your items are clean and organized, but if you experience having some out-of-control issues regarding your routines, you could have symptoms of OCD. Being obsessed with counting is also a common symptom of OCD; teens count because they feel that somehow certain numbers hold a significance. For example, someone with OCD may not own only one certain style/color of shoe, but if 9 is their lucky number, they will have 9 pairs of them lined up nice and neat in a row in their closet. They may count aloud, or just mentally, but will count things like cracks in the sidewalk, how many people they pass in the hallway wearing yellow, or how many schoolbooks people are carrying.

People suffering from OCD can't help having intrusive thoughts because they are uncontrollable. Someone with OCD may have an obsession about dirt and germs, so they feel they need to wash their hands more frequently than the norm. If you have ever double-checked a locked door, imagine that someone suffering from OCD can spend hours double-checking, rearranging, and counting things. It's probably not surprising to find that many OCD sufferers are also hoarders.

As with many of the anxiety disorders, OCD often takes place late in the teen years and can be influenced by heredity. According to Jason Porterfield (2014), OCD can also be caused as a result of abnormal brain circuitry and infection by the same virus that causes strep infections.

People suffering from OCD may have some common obsessions like:

- A fear of dirt, germs, viruses
- A fear of losing control
- A fear of accidentally hurting someone because of carelessness
- A fear of not being perfect at everything
- A fear of losing a cherished object
- A need for order and symmetry with common objects at home or school
- A preoccupation with special numbers or particular words

Everyone develops their own special way of doing things and it's important to notice that some hobbies and interests may overlap with OCD symptoms, but are not in fact signs of OCD. For example, if you collect sports cards, coins, or stamps, this is not a sign of OCD. This is also true if you are a teen that is a huge fan of Doctor Who and your response to every catastrophe is to reverse the polarity of the neutron flow." That doesn't mean you have OCD, you are just a nerd.

Sufferers of OCD are easy to spot and can also be diagnosed with depression or other anxiety orders. According to Angus Whyte (2020), a typical course of treatment involves Cognitive Behavioral Therapy (CBT), which is an effective approach to OCD. While the symptoms of OCD may never totally fade, they can be managed, and the victims of OCD can go on to lead healthy and productive lives.

Social Anxiety Disorder

Being shy about social events when you are a teen is normal, but if you begin to display nervousness over everyday social situations at school, with family, or with friends, you could be experiencing symptoms of social anxiety disorder. If you worry about being judged negatively by others or you constantly have feelings of fear and avoidance, it may be time to consider you may have an anxiety disorder.

Anyone suffering from social anxiety disorder will find any social setting torturous, and they may even avoid eating or drinking in public for fear of being observed and criticized. Because of the nature of this disorder, sufferers will find it extremely difficult to develop friendships or have relationships of any kind. A person suffering from social anxiety disorder will go to any length to avoid a social situation so they will not experience rejection or embarrassment that goes way beyond the limits of mere shyness. Symptoms of social anxiety disorder can include:

- A fear of social interaction
- Overwhelming self-consciousness
- A fear of judgment
- Intense worry about anything revolving around social situations
- Complete avoidance of social situations
- Withdrawal
- Isolation
- A fear of humiliation/embarrassment
- Nausea, trembling, sweating, or blushing

Specific Phobia

Phobias all on their own can cause panic attacks and a strong desire to avoid something. A specific phobia centers around a certain object or situation that you feel you have an extreme fear of. If you have an inherent fear of men who wear hats in the house or, like Indiana Jones, you fear snakes, you could have a specific phobia. When you demonstrate a specific phobia to an object, you are expressing an irrational fear of something that causes no real threat. Some common phobias include:

- Flying in airplanes
- Fear of heights
- Fear of enclosed spaces
- Fear of the dark
- Fear of blood
- Fear of certain animals, insects, or spiders
- Fear of clowns

When you are triggered by a phobia, you tend to avoid situations that put you in the line of fire. Depending on what you are avoiding, it can impact your daily life and put limitations on your very existence. For example, you could have a fear of flying in airplanes, but you get a great job offer once you graduate that includes a lot of travel. You are going to miss out on a fantastic opportunity to advance your life, all due to your phobia.

Interestingly, the phobias that develop during childhood tend to fade, but if they develop as a teen or an adult, they often become persistent and have lasting effects.

Substance-Induce Anxiety Disorder

The symptoms of this disorder are characterized by feelings of intense anxiety or panic caused by alcohol, drugs, or medications. Feelings of anxiety can be felt during exposure or the withdrawal from the initial exposure.

Often, mistakes are made by using drugs or other means to try and boost confidence, help with relaxation, and lower inhibitions, and people don't realize that the anxiety they may be experiencing is because of the substances. After all, those substances are supposed to be making us feel good, right?

If you are seeking a diagnosis from your healthcare provider, your doctor will check to ensure that the anxiety you are experiencing wasn't there before the use of the substance in question.

In addition to drugs, medications, and unknown substances, you may be surprised to learn that caffeine/energy drinks can also induce anxiety disorder. When caffeine is consumed in large amounts, it can cause mild to moderate anxiety. According to MedlinePlus (2020), the consumption of energy beverages has been associated with high-risk behavior such as marijuana use, fighting, taking risks, alcohol abuse, and drug abuse.

According to the Center for Substance Abuse Treatment (2005), substance-induced disorders include:

- Delirium. Described as being confused, seeing or hearing things that don't exist, or the inability to recognize people.
- Dementia. Symptoms of this disorder include forgetfulness and reduced thinking abilities that interfere with daily routines.
- Amnestic disorder. This disorder involves a loss of memory or the inability to create new memories or learn new information.
- Psychotic disorder. In this condition, a person can suffer from hallucinations, be agitated, and babble incoherently. Typically a person afflicted with this isn't aware of their behavior.
- Mood disorder. When someone suffers from mood disorder. they can experience long periods of extreme sorrow, happiness, or both.
- Anxiety disorder. This disorder can cause an individual to experience a lack of concentration, unwanted thoughts, or a fear of impending doom.
- Perceptual disorder. If someone suffers from this disorder, they find they have difficulties perceiving the nature of an object or using their sensory organs.
- Sleep disorder. See chapter 7 for a list of sleep disorders.

Post Traumatic Stress Disorder (PTSD)

We have all heard about soldiers who come back from war and are plagued by PTSD. The symptoms of PTSD include trouble concentrating, panic attacks, problems falling or staying asleep, and restlessness. PTSD is typically precipitated by an event which has caused harm, been upsetting, or triggered a terrifying event.

But teens can also suffer from the effects of PTSD. The memories of any traumatic event can cause lingering memories of being overwhelmed, such as abuse, car accidents, or being trapped in a burning building. Terrible memories can be triggered by something as simple as a look on someone's face or a cologne they may be wearing.

Just because you can be any age and have a traumatizing event doesn't mean that you will get PTSD. Some people are just more resilient than others when dealing with catastrophes.

Toxic stressors can change the way your body functions and you may feel emotionally or physically exhausted. So if you are dealing with violence in your home or school, or you have a parent, family member, or close friend abusing substances, these events can prove difficult for you to work through.

After the first month of an event, the symptoms of PTSD may start to develop, but it can begin months or even years later and can be triggered by an event similar to the memory. Even the anniversary of an event can cause the dam to break and you can experience flashbacks.

Someone with PTSD might have one or a combination of the following symptoms:

- Anxiety. Anyone suffering from PTSD can be easily startled or may appear tense. They will have difficulty concentrating and sleeping.
- Emotional numbness. A person with PTSD can feel numb or detached. They can look at the world and see only the negativity. They experience difficulties putting their trust in anyone or anything.
- Avoiding reminders of the original trauma. Anyone suffering from the effects of PTSD may choose to avoid activities, places, or people that remind them of the stressful event. Usually, they will avoid talking about the event to anyone.
- Reliving the traumatic event. PTSD can cause ugly flashbacks, nightmares, and disturbing mental images surrounding the original trauma.

Traumatic events are very common in our culture, so you shouldn't feel that you have been singled out if you struggled with PTSD. PTSD is an understandable reaction in the face of some very difficult events.

If you are troubled by any of the anxiety disorders we have discussed in this section, you should talk to your parents, counselor, or healthcare professional immediately. If you are reaching out to get help with your struggles, please know that you are extremely courageous. There are people out there who can help, and you shouldn't have to go through this alone.

Case Study: Iris

"I first met Christopher when I was a freshman in high school and I thought I had found true love. During the first year of our relationship he was sweet and caring, but when our sophomore year got underway he began to change. He started with some verbal abuse, saying things like I was ugly and that no one would ever be able to love me. He convinced me and I bought into it hook, line, and sinker. I started to be grateful that he would even be bothered with me. After a short amount of time, Christopher began to hit me as well and he was always so angry. I was constantly accused of flirting with other boys and I deserved everything I got. I spent a lot of time alone in my room crying because I believed everything he said and I felt intense hatred for myself.

"I never told anyone, because I believed everything he said. That somehow, I was at fault for his loss of control. When my parents found out, they shipped me off to an out-of-state college. At first, I thought my parents shared Christopher's views and sent me away because I deserved it. Later I figured out that they sent me so I could make a new start with new people. But it didn't start out that way. When I was alone and studying, I would sometimes have very vivid memories of Christopher hitting, yelling, and shaming me. One day in class, there was a new boy sitting next to me and his cologne smelled just like the kind Christopher used to wear.

"I skipped the next class and ran back to my dorm room, trembling. I couldn't stop crying. I barely knew my roommate at the time, but she had seemed like a kind person. She was shocked when she returned to our room and found me curled up in a dark

69

corner. From the look on her face, I just knew that I could trust her.

"Tilly became my best friend, we spent all our spare time together attending her yoga class, and she shared her guided meditation tapes with me. I had a whole new world open up for me and I began to realize that I was worthy. Looking back with what I know now, I can't help but think that Christopher may have had some abuse going on at his own home and his way of dealing with it was to pass his anger along to me. At least, this is what made the most amount of sense. Every week I feel stronger and I finally have self-esteem back. It took a very long time, but I have Tilly to thank for it. I think she saved my life that day."

Exercise: Emotional Awareness

This meditation draws upon your mindful awareness. By following this mindful practice, you are able to create a new way to experience and deal with emotions. Individuals focus too much on the emotion but discount how it feels within our bodies. When using mindfulness, we can develop a new understanding about our emotions.

1. Find a comfortable seated position or lie on your back (you may need to place a pillow behind your knees). What's important is that your spine is kept straight, your chest is open, and your eyes are closed.
2. Ground yourself. The best way to accomplish this is to focus on the flow created by five or six deep breaths.

3. Once you feel centered, you can ask yourself questions. Do you find an emotion lurking here?
4. If you do acknowledge that there is an emotion present such as anger, confusion, irritation, anxiety, or grief, can you feel that the emotion has become present within your body? You may feel some sensations such as:
   - Tightness
   - Pressure
   - Twisting
   - Heat
   - Coldness
   - Throbbing
   - Lightness
   - Heaviness
   - Tingling
5. While remaining in your mindful state, observe this emotion and take note of any sensation you feel associated with it. Your mind may develop a story associated with this experience. Should this happen, you want to journey back to the first raw experience of the physical sensation.
6. Spend a few minutes studying the physical presentation of your emotion. You can take longer; just do whatever feels comfortable for you.
7. Release yourself from the mindfulness session and return now to deep breaths to ground yourself. Take your time, and when you are ready, open your eyes slowly.

Mindfulness is the key to achieving control over your anxieties. Peaceful exercises help you to become more thoughtful and understanding of both yourself and others. Those who suffer from high emotions such as anxiety, stress, panic, and fear frequently experience these unwanted emotions without knowing where they came from or how best to handle them. If you aren't happy with the direction you are headed in, change it in a mindful way.

Managing Stress, Anxiety, and Fear

It doesn't matter how busy someone is, how many responsibilities they face, or demands that are made upon them, the amount of stress and anxiety can be managed. Unfortunately, there is no single magical approach that can solve everything with a flick of a wand. Anxiety in teens often comes with symptoms of feeling out of control, on edge, and loaded up with worry.

Just as stress and anxiety create different responses in you, different techniques will vary in their results from person to person. Any outlet that provides you with a chance to relax and take a break from your stress will be beneficial. You can pick anything from gardening to tai chi, as long as you find it relaxing.

There are many ways to cope with your stress and anxiety that are beneficial, so we would like you to box up all those thoughts of unhealthy coping and let's look at some healthy ways of starting small and ending up with big-time changes.

Nip Negativity

If you are beginning to think negatively as you are reading this, let's start there and nip that negativity in the bud.

- *"I don't feel like I'm worth it."* = *"Everyone is worthy of respect and love."*
- *"I deserve what happened to me."* = *"I deserve care."*
- *"I don't feel I can change."* = *"I can learn new skills."*

When you begin to make changes, start small and don't get discouraged. It most likely took a long time to develop what bothers you, so it will take some time to unravel. You can begin by doing some easy tasks.

- Watch a funny movie. It's always uplifting to watch a movie that is so funny you can't help but smile and laugh.
- Read a book that interests you. Make sure that you pick something that isn't related to schoolwork or your anxiety.
- Do something creative. Ever wanted to paint a design on something for your room? Try it!
- Take a walk. Better yet, snap a harness and leash on Sparky and take him with you. Observe your dog, because they live in the moment and they can be very good teachers. While you are on your walk, try to focus on just your walk because there is a lot out there around you to take in.

- Play a game. It doesn't matter if it's solitaire alone or a family game of Monopoly. Even the concentration required by putting together a puzzle can be enjoyable.
- Write a short story or a poem.
- Play a sport you enjoy.
- Try to have some fun. It doesn't matter if it is with family or friends!
- Talk to your parents, counselor, or close friends about what is bothering you.

Tip: Watch Those Words

Sometimes the word that you choose can have an effect on your emotions, mood, and your physical well-being. Try to make word choices that make your language more supportive. For example:

- Instead of "difficult," try "challenging."
- Instead of always telling yourself that you are tired, tell yourself you are a warrior.
- Instead of saying that you aren't good at something, replace it with "I'm still learning this."

You can also add the word "yet" at the end of something to make yourself a promise!

- I can't solve this problem, yet.
- I physically cannot do this, yet.
- I do not understand the math, yet.

Get the idea? Of course you do!

Sit back and take some time to journal about the changes that you are making in your life to help you cope with your stress or anxiety. By starting to participate in healthier habits, you are declaring yourself worthy. And you are! To become resilient is a skill that you can develop just like any other skill. Take note of all your strengths and build upon them.

Break Out Your Journal!

Journaling is a fantastic way to express yourself. While on your exploration, you can find meaning surrounding your past, relish the present, and develop untold inspiration for your future.

Practicing journaling can offer you excellent health benefits, and when combined with meditation, you may find the effects doubled. If you feel uneasy by sitting still in silence to practice traditional meditation, then you may find that putting a pen to paper is an excellent substitute. If you feel that you have a busy mind, then writing may provide just the engagement that you have been looking for. The act of journaling can open doors to self-awareness in the same way as mindful meditation.

If you already practice mindful meditation, then you will be able to enhance the effects by writing immediately after your routine session. By being expressive in your journal entries, you will be able to manage stress, build self-esteem, and reduce anxiety. At the same time, your written words can help develop better concentration and improve focus.

With practice, you will be able to combine expression into your writing and help replace any self-criticism, anger, or harsh judgment with kind thoughts, expressions full of beauty, and hope, while adding a bit of whimsy to your life.

The best way to establish a journaling routine is to establish some topics that you can rotate and use frequently. You may want to set aside a window of time each day, but you can also keep a pad of paper and a pen by your bedside for times when you cannot fall asleep at night and you can write down any worries to clear your mind before bedtime.

Mornings tend to be the best time to journal, but you may not be able to fit that in with the mad dash to class each day. If you have time, jot down your dreams or worries about the day ahead. You may even find that you are a budding author!

Examples of Journaling Ideas

1. Reflect on your past summer and write about any adventures you had. How did these experiences make you stronger and/or smarter? Were you able to relax during your adventure? What can you do to continually experience those feelings of calm?
2. Pick a season. For our example, let's choose autumn. What are your favorite things to do during the autumn season? What do you look forward to the most? What does fall mean to you?
3. Friendship. Who is your oldest friend, and when and where did you meet them? How has your friendship

changed over the years? Why do you believe your friendship has lasted this long?

4. It's all about me! Name three things you do just for yourself regularly. Now, add three things that you want to start doing.

5. Focus on the fun! List five things that made you smile today and why.

6. Never fear new things. What are five activities you would like to try but have always intimidated you? Of those five, which will you try first?

7. Notice all the small stuff! When you look back on your day, what was good about your morning? What was your favorite taste sensation for the day? What music did you listen to?

Don't Forget About Doodling

Don't discount the benefit of a good doodle either. If you don't have anything for a day or two that you want to write about, consider merely doodling to keep your mind grounded. You don't need to stress about what subject you doodle; merely close your eyes and let your hand fall where it may. This can help release any inhibitions you have about doodling. Remember that there are no rules and you are only doodling for yourself, so there is no one you are trying to impress. If you find an image that soothes you, you can even choose to draw it repeatedly. Just pick something that brings you joy. As a teen, I used to doodle poodles and I found it fun and peaceful. There are many famous people who have doodled over the years, so you would be in good company:

- President Dwight D. Eisenhower
- President John F. Kennedy
- President Ronald Regan
- Beatle John Lennon
- Artist Pablo Picasso

People have very short attention spans, so while you are looking at your phone, talking, and changing channels on your Roku®, Amazon Firestick®, or Apple TV, remember that our culture is very fast-paced. Just keep in mind that the mind and body do not get over trauma quickly, even if the lady on the Netflix show achieved it in one episode. That's Hollywood and you are a real, living, breathing person. Be kind and make sure you aren't expecting forty-five minute miracles. It can be a challenge, but you will need to try and view your situation in a more balanced way. Remember that you are not to blame for being the victim. Healing takes time.

You can identify your supportive friends by writing down the names of people you know you can trust. This list may include others your own age, but you may have some adults on there too. When you look at the names you have written down, what made you choose them? Are they overall kind to others? Have you seen them helping others with their problems? Did they open up to you about something personal?

Meditation and mindfulness helps you to accept what has happened to you. What we mean is that you certainly don't have to like what has happened, but you wouldn't want to repeat it either. Your acceptance means that you will eventually come to understand the traumatic event isn't something that you had control over and are unable to change. No one can change the past, but that doesn't mean that the past will define your future. Teens have their whole life in front of them, so there is time to create a new and improved story for your life. Gift yourself patience so that you can create a brighter future.

Identifying What Causes Your Stress

Let's see if you can find some things on this list that stress you out:

- Your family. There can be many difficult scenarios within your family life. Maybe your parents are arguing, separating, or even contemplating divorce. Maybe they are arguing with one of your siblings, or even you.
- School. There are also several possibilities that create stress at school—for example, your exams, grades, difficulties with a teacher, difficulties with other students like bullying, or experiencing learning problems.
- Friendships or your social circle. This can include a loss of a friend, someone asking you to keep a secret that you are uncomfortable with, or disagreements with friends.

- Body image. You could be concerned about your height, weight, skin blemishes, ethnicity, or a combination of these.
- Romantic relationships. Are you in a new relationship and just not feeling confident? Maybe you are in a complicated relationship or one that just broke up?
- Bullying or cyberbullying. It will be stressful if someone is constantly humiliating you in front of others or making you a target of hurtful comments. There is a lot of this going on through social media. A person who dislikes you or something you spoke out about hunts down your page and criticizes you.
- Peer pressure. This could be teens you go to school with or someone in your social circle. They may be trying to pressure you to use drugs, drink alcohol, or take unwise risks.
- Money. Perhaps you or your family have little means and there isn't much money to go around. It can be difficult to buy books, pay for new clothes, or attend school functions. It may be stressful and embarrassing if you have trouble fitting in with your group of friends.
- Dealing with a change. Perhaps you have moved to a different state and are starting out all over with a new school or making new friends. If you have lost a grandparent, parent, pet, or close friend, these could all be stressors.

Some of these things you will have no control over, but you do have control over how you respond to them. For example, you may have to follow your family in a move and it could be quite far from your previous home.

Think about a stressful situation that has happened to you and how you responded. Do you wish you had reacted differently?

Stress doesn't always just happen, it can be built up over time. Are there any stressors you have experienced that are not represented on this list?

The ability to face your fear is probably one of the toughest challenges you will face, but you do not have to face everything at once. When you begin to confront a fear, you begin by learning ways to relax your mind and body. If you can relax your body, the mind will follow suit.

The simplest way to calm your body down is to learn to breathe. What's that? You say you already know how to breathe because you do it all day every day? Well, that is true, but there are other ways to breathe. Deep breathing is breathing from your diaphragm. Most people breathe using their upper lungs, but the way to a deep "belly breath," is to breathe from the lower part of your lungs or the diaphragm.

People who play instruments like the trumpet, trombone, or French horn learn to breathe from their diaphragm because they need the breath support to produce sounds from their horns. Also people who are trained in opera or classical singing always breathe from their diaphragm so that they can project to the back of the theater and sustain those long notes.

When you become anxious or fearful, your breathing responds by becoming shallow and quick. Here's how to learn belly breathing:

- Begin by finding a comfortable place to lie down. If you want, you can place a small pillow under both your head and your knees for comfort.
- Place one hand on your upper chest and the other below your ribcage. If your diaphragm is engaged, then the hand on your upper chest should remain mostly still. The other hand will allow you to feel your diaphragm as you breathe.
- Breath in slowly through your nose, taking the time to fill your diaphragm with air. While you do this, you should feel your stomach rise. Do not try to force or push your abdominal muscles outward. Your airflow should remain smooth.
- Now breathe out through your mouth slowly. Your belly should fall as you exhale. Take care not to force your stomach area inward or clench any muscles.

If you are finding this exercise difficult to perform, it may be that you have been breathing with only your chest.

If you can maintain a healthy lifestyle, it can help you to reduce the effects that stress and anxiety can have on your life. Mindful eating can help you establish a healthy diet that provides you with not only the nutrition you require, but also includes listening to your body.

When you practice mindful eating, you will recognize your body telling you that you are full. It can also let you know when more fuel is required by growling at us. Just like when you establish sleeping habits, you should also apply that to eating habits. Regular times and places should be set to keep your body on schedule to receive the fuel that it needs.

Make sure that the diet you are following is a healthy one. Your regular meals should include fruits, vegetables, and other nutrients to keep your body supplied with needed vitamins and minerals. Stress can deplete your natural resources, so it is important that you stay on top of your needs and listen to your cravings. If you suddenly are dying to have an orange, your body must need it. There are some stress-reducing foods that are helpful for your system and they include grains such as whole wheat bread or oatmeal. Make sure you eat those leafy greens that you find in salads and vegetables such as squash and peppers. Avocados and oranges are beneficial along with fish that contain omega-3 fatty acids, like salmon or tuna. Giving in to the temptation of junk food will only make you feel worse.

Exercising is a great way to reduce your levels of stress, but we don't mean you have to go out right away and run five miles or become an expert on the uneven bars in an afternoon. Low-impact exercising is the best type of workout you can do and it will boost your mood and help your immunity. In addition to getting your systems moving, exercise will also assist you in the relief of muscle tension created by stress. So whether you choose to talk some walks, practice yoga, or learn tai chi, the physical movement will help you clear your mind.

Activities

There are two ways that are recommended to work on managing your anxiety, practicing prevention and practicing intervention.

When you practice prevention, it means you should spend time every day practicing relaxation techniques. When you feel your anxiety level on the rise, you perform a relaxation technique that helps you to calm down and that is what is referred to as practicing intervention.

Some people don't understand why they should be practicing prevention relaxation techniques before they feel anxious. The benefit is clear; by practicing your relaxation techniques every day, you can be better prepared to prevent anxiety from forming. The ability to practice intervention can help you reduce the anxiety and calm yourself.

Get out a piece of paper and something to write with. Make two columns; name one "prevention," and the other one "intervention." Below is a list of activities, put them in the appropriate columns.

- Study for a test
- Remember information studied during the test
- Eat an assortment of healthy foods daily
- Drink fluids when you have a cold
- In order to avoid an accident, slam on your brakes
- Drive at the posted speed limit
- Save a portion of your allowance/paycheck weekly
- Ask your parents for money when you need it
- Put gas in your car when the gauge reads half-full
- Put gas in a can and walk to your car, which is stalled because it ran out of gas
- Bring a healthy snack in your backpack in case you feel hungry
- Buy junk food out of the vending machine when you suddenly get hungry

- Get your books back to the library before the due date
- Return your library books a day late and pay a fine

After assigning these to a column, let's ask a few more questions.

- Write down three instances within the past week that you considered to be prevention.
- Now write down three times in the same past week that you think could be considered intervention.
- Which one of your three interventions might have had better results if you had practiced prevention instead?
- Describe any activities you already practice as prevention to keep your anxiety level from getting too high.
- Write down steps you take to help yourself when your anxiety level takes off.

Be Self-Compassionate

Through our journey of life, we need to refrain from being self-critical. It's a common problem when you become your own worst critic, but it can be overcome. If we allow the voices in our heads to run wild, we can make them kind and supportive, or destructive and devaluing. How you change this, is to choose to view yourself with self-compassion. Accept that you aren't perfect because, frankly, no one is. The best way to view your errors is to recognize the potential for growth and learning from every mistake. There are five essential steps to build your self-compassion.

1. Practice forgiveness. Stop punishing yourself! Raking yourself over the proverbial hot coals is not going to help you grow. Even if you did something that wasn't your best work, leave yourself a note reminding you to be gentle and kind to yourself. Learn to grow from your mistakes and as Elsa says in Frozen, "Let it go!"

2. Develop a growth mindset. If you are always entering a challenge with the belief that it is impossible, then where is your opportunity to grow? Embrace your challenges with a smile on your face and a song in your heart. Never give up!

3. Feel gratitude. It can be difficult to remember what we have, instead of what we don't. Consider keeping a gratitude journal and write down the blessings that you often overlook.

4. Be generous. Generosity can be a powerful way of employing compassion. What style of reciprocity do you practice? Are you a matcher, taker, or a giver? If you are overly generous, you may need to take your own well-being into account, but doing good things for others will make you happy.

5. Be mindful. The act of mindfulness has a positive impact on self-compassion. Attempt to always be in the moment. However, do it without judgment. When a feeling arises, whether positive or negative, allow it to have its moment in the sun, and then let it go.

Everyone is worthy of love and respect. Recognize your strengths.

Self-compassion is necessary to help you heal from any anxieties or insecurities. To assist you in acceptance of yourself, try using the below worksheet. You can make this significantly longer, I have just entered an example on line one. You can personalize your entries.

Self-Compassion Worksheets

1. Competencies

Helpful Competencies at Home	Helpful Competencies at School	Helpful Competencies in My Social Group
I help out with household chores.	I help my friends study for difficult tests.	I created a book club for like-minded friends.

2. Perceptions

Misperceptions	Reshaping Perceptions
I will never be able to complete my schoolwork on time.	If I employ effective time management, this can help me complete my schoolwork on time. I got this!

3. Motivation

Make a List of Activities That Increase Your Motivation
Take a nature walk
Write music

Chapter 4: Coping With Depression Using Meditation

"You can have wounds that trap your very soul in purgatory, but none can tell the racking pain that has invaded your world unless you let them in." – August Benjamin, Theologian

Depression is not who you are or what you will experience all the time. Everyone experiences feeling blue from time to time, and throughout our lives we all encounter sadness, stress, and trauma. The pain you feel with depression is a real thing, and feeling sad for more than a few weeks could spell depression for an individual. While you are suffering from depression, it feels like everything you touch is permeated with darkness. Nothing seems to work out, and you can spiral even further into the dark abyss.

Keep communication open between you and your parents. Teen depression can be quite different from how adult depression is displayed. As a result, adults don't often recognize the signs of depression in teens.

Keep a written diary of symptoms you may be experiencing so that you can discuss them with your parents. Discussing depression is no different than talking about a physical health problem you would experience. Remember that your depression can look a lot like mood swings to your parents or guardians.

No teens are exempt from depression because it doesn't distinguish based on popularity, race, gender, or academic successes. Depression doesn't care if someone is a star athlete or a standout on the chess team, so keeping communication channels open is very important. Teens can often become more irritable than sad when depressed, which is why adults may miss your symptoms. Because of this, teen depression may not be addressed in time, or at all.

Depression can cover a lot of ground, but there are four main types that affect teens.

Adjustment Disorder

In other words, you may be struggling while adjusting to a change like divorce, moving, being bullied, the death of a loved one or a beloved pet, or changing schools. An adjustment disorder can present other symptoms such as showing anxiety, having a depressed mood, a mix of both depression and anxiety, or a disturbance of conduct. These can show up in teens as crying spells, feelings of hopelessness, separation anxiety, or becoming defiant and getting into fights.

Dysthymia

More commonly referred to as persistent depressive disorder, dysthymia is a chronic depression that lasts for over a year. If you are a teen experiencing this, you may feel irritable, have low self-esteem, experience low energy, and have bouts of hopelessness. Dysthymia can interfere with eating and sleeping habits, concentration, and affect decision-making. Because of the length of dysthymia, a teen's life can get set back on learning and socialization.

Bipolar Disorder

If you feel that you have depression and then experience a continued period of intense energy, racing thoughts and over-the-top behaviors, you could be experiencing a manic episode. These periods can also include hallucinations or delusional behavior. Unfortunately, sleep problems and bipolar disorder tend to feed off each other, making conditions worsen. Symptoms include a reduction in sleep, difficulties focusing, and a wicked short temper.

Major Depression

Major depression is our last and most serious form of depression. Major depression symptoms include a persistent, invading sadness, irritability, and considering suicide. If at any time you have thoughts of suicide, please contact the National Suicide Prevention Lifeline at: 1-800-273-8255.

According to Steven Gans, MD (2020), a survey conducted on teen depression showed that as much as eight percent of teens experience depression each year. Because depression can lead to problems in the home, difficulties at school, and a lack of interest in life, it is very important to check in with a medical professional before symptoms can get out of hand.

"My home life was a disaster, for some reason my parents thought a new location and new start would improve things. For me, that wasn't the case and even though school was an escape, I was always full of gloom. I was a loner at school because I was always unkempt and no one wanted to be my partner in any class. My big brother wasn't handling things the same way that I was. He seemed to be popular and had lots of friends quickly after we moved in. I finally asked him about it, because I was tired of not having any friends. He told me that he had read a book once on practicing positivity. Basically, he told me I had to start believing in the positive and making changes to reflect that. He told me that people always wanted to be friends with a positive, kind person and that I should do a makeover on myself. So I started making eye contact with people instead of looking down at the floor. I took the time to make sure my clothes were relatively free of wrinkles and I double-checked to make sure I had actually combed my hair every day. It took time to develop, but I have always been a stubborn kid. While I have made a few good friends, I am still working on being more positive about myself. I even went out for the soccer team and I found out that I am pretty darn good at it." – Bill, 15

Read over our list below and write down any of these symptoms you seem to be experiencing. Make notes on any of them that you may have input on.

- Have you noticed any physical or medical issues that have turned up recently for no apparent reason? Digestive issues, aches, or pains that never seem to go away despite any treatments applied to them can be a sign of depression.
- Do you seem to have lost all your energy? If your normal tasks seem to be zapping your energy, leaving you feeling

tired and run-down, this could be attributed to depression.

- Are you experiencing a loss of appetite or a sudden increase in appetite? Ask yourself, are you eating in order to cope?
- Are you experiencing abnormal sleep patterns? It is possible that you are finding the weight of the world intolerable and just want to sleep all the time. You could also be experiencing disruptions in your sleep, like insomnia. Do you have trouble falling asleep and staying asleep?
- Do you seem to have slowed down to a crawl or perhaps become uneasy?
- Are you losing your self-esteem and self-worth? It's possible that you are feeling hopeless or unworthy. Teens that are experiencing bouts of depression believe that they are a bad person.
- Have you been using negative self-talk? We all can experience negative self-talk, but excessive amounts can create stress and have effects on your mind, body, and soul. Examples of negative self-talk are "I can't do anything right" or "I'm just not good at anything." Negative self-talk when coupled with depression can be quite damaging for an individual.
- Do you struggle to find the bright side in anything? Depression has a way of turning everything in our lives negative. Ask yourself if you are struggling to see any positives in your day-to-day life. Bullying or social exclusion. If you are finding that you are a target of bullying, remember that they prey on others that suffer from self-negativity.

- Are you finding that you are sensitive to criticism? Sometimes depression can lead to students avoiding activities where they fear they may fail. The reverse can also be true if you find that you have suddenly become a perfectionist, trying to avert being rejected or criticized.
- Teens with depression can either withdraw from their friends or change their social group. Have you suddenly changed which crowd you hang out with, and are they the wrong crowd?
- Have you tried to hide in the online world? Often teens will create a different persona and enter chats or role-playing games where they can be anyone but themselves.
- A teen experiencing depression can feel empty and often burst into tears because of the sadness they are going through.
- Have you turned your back on your favorite things? Depression can often cause a person to lose interest in activities and hobbies that were previously enjoyable.
- Are you finding that you are having trouble concentrating or forgetting to do daily tasks? Depression can deprive you of your ability to concentrate. It can leave your brain in a fog.
- Do small things that you would normally overlook suddenly annoy you? Depression can increase restlessness and irritability.
- Are you experiencing a decline in your grades? Some students are able to maintain their grade point average, but depression can be a factor in a sudden decline in grades.
- Genetics. Depression can run in families.
- Have you ever, no matter how fleeting, given thought to

death, or thoughts of suicide?

If any of these symptoms seemed like problems you are facing, know that you are not alone. There are some successful and famous people out there who have faced depression and came back stronger than they were before.

- Actors: Christian Bale, Angelina Jolie, Dwayne "The Rock" Johnson, Gwyneth Paltrow, and Harrison Ford
- Artists: Henri Matisse and Jackson Pollock
- Athletes: Michael Phelps, Amanda Beard, Justin Duchscherer, Ricky Williams, Serena Williams, Dan Carcillo, and Oscar De La Hoya
- Authors: Stephen King and J.K. Rowling
- Billionaire businessman: Ted Turner
- Classical music composers: Wolfgang Mozart and Ludwig van Beethoven
- Musicians: Adele, Bruce Springsteen, Naomi Judd, and Zendaya
- Physicist: Sir Isaac Newton
- US presidents: Abraham Lincoln, John Adams, and Calvin Coolidge

It Only Takes 10 Minutes

Who doesn't want to gain better control of their thoughts? What if I were to tell you that in just 10 minutes each day you can alter the structure of your brain for the better? Yes, it is possible to rewire your brain with new, healthier structure. Using mindfulness-based treatment comes with significantly lower risks of returning to depression because of the power of change. Mindfulness allows you to pay attention to your thoughts and feelings without becoming entangled in negative triggers. Mindfulness can also help you to pinpoint early signs of depression and treat those symptoms. Take 10 minutes to explore mindfulness!

1. For 10 seconds, focus on your breathing.
2. As you breathe in and out, pay close attention to any sensations within your body.
3. Don't put a good or bad label on the sensation, merely try to describe it to yourself. For example, you may feel your heartbeat speed up or slow down, your chest could feel tight, etc.

And mindfulness is just that simple! There are no complicated instructions to follow and there is no equipment to buy. (Unless you just want a soft pillow to sit on!) Mindfulness helps you with everyday situations and you can do it seated, taking a walk, or lying down comfortably. With mindfulness, you pay attention to right now, without any judgment and you can do this in five easy steps.

1. Focus on only the present moment and let everything else disappear. What kinds of sounds or smells do you notice?
2. Pass no judgment.
3. Become distracted by your thoughts, don't worry, every human mind does this.
4. When you find yourself inevitably distracted, bring your focus back to the present.
5. Repeat all these steps.

If you suffer from depression, mindfulness will help you become more aware of your thought processes. With this tool, you can choose what you pay attention to.

Mindful Steps To Help Relieve Depression

Depression can be challenging, and while under its influence, you may think it is an insurmountable journey, but it all begins with that first step. Using mindfulness, you can reconnect with your values and learn to live in the present moment while having a vision and a purpose. Using a confidence worksheet, try rating your confidence levels using the below ratings. By doing so, you can measure your strengths and weaknesses so you know which areas you need to focus more mindfulness efforts on.

- Needs more help - 1, 2, 3
- Somewhat confident - 4, 5, 6
- Confident - 7, 8
- You got this! - 9, 10

Step	Confidence Level
The Ability To Use the Present Moment as Your Anchor	
The Ability To Practice Nonjudgmental Acceptance	
The Ability To Detach and Let Go	
The Ability To Practice Self-Compassion	
Vision and Intention	
Make and Keep Promises	

What Are Your Depression Triggers?

Depression can make you vulnerable, but until you rate how much it affects you, you may not understand how things apply to your life. You can use these examples, or make up some of your own. The idea is to rate how large of a problem you are facing. 1 is for no problem and 10 is for an extremely large issue. In the final column, indicate if the issue is past or present. Perhaps it could be both.

Trigger	Rating on a Scale (1 to 10)	Problem (recent or past)
I feel tired often and never get enough sleep		
I rely on substances more often than I should		
I constantly worry about finances		
I suffer from a lot of poor health		
I struggle with memories of abuse		
I am under pressure at school		
I am under pressure at home		
I have conflicts with my parents		
I feel that my friends merely use me		

After you complete this chart, take a look at your final answers. Did you mark most of your triggers as a 1 or 2? Do your numbers represent emotional turmoil? Are your triggers from the past or are they more recent? And have they been persisting over a long period of time?

Remember that problems create painful feelings and the longer these are allowed to influence your life, the greater risk you run. Once you have identified your biggest obstacles, you will be able to take an action that resonates best with you. Everyone has their own method of dealing with their particular challenges. Whether that is talking to a close friend or family member or perhaps planning your own steps you plan to take to be actionable in a resolution. You must do what makes you comfortable when resolving issues that previously created depression.

Do You Run on Autopilot?

Sometimes depression is caused by always running on autopilot. When suffering from depression, you can experience worry, boredom, or an inability to relax. How many of these apply to you?

1. I am bored most of the time.
2. I seem to waste a lot of time surfing the internet or watching TV without really having a destination.
3. I feel that I am not allowed to relax.
4. I often am unable to sit still and find anything to keep me busy.
5. I rarely feel emotion.
6. I feel disconnected.
7. I am bored frequently.
8. I am always focusing on what's ahead instead of before me.
9. I always feel rushed and am constantly behind.
10. I find when I am talking with someone I lose my focus and stop paying attention.
11. I put off activities that would likely create enjoyment.
12. I often lose concentration on things that I am doing.
13. I often become irritated when my daily schedule becomes disrupted.
14. Instead of joy, I just feel numb.

Study what you circled and identify if these are autopilot behaviors. If so, they may be setting you up for continued depression. Now that you have identified your issues, you can use mindfulness to create a better life.

Account for Emotional Avoidance

We all have things that go wrong, but choose a recent event or interaction that didn't go well for you, leaving you more depressed. Right now, take time to write about that situation and what actions you took regarding it. What was your final outcome? Looking back, could you have come up with better, more effective, and positive actions?

Situation:

Action:

Action:

Action:

Action:

Final Outcome: (For example, did it trigger negative emotional reactions, did you feel worse?)

Better Action:

Better Action:

Better Action:

Better Action:

By practicing mindfulness, you don't react immediately, and by doing, so you allow yourself time to respond positively.

Exercises

Draw a Picture of Depression

Let's try a mindfulness exercise! We will call it drawing a picture of depression.

Imagine that depression is sitting next to you in that empty chair. Try and picture what depression looks like. If you have seen the Harry Potter movies, do you remember when a Boggart took on the student's worst fear and Harry saw a dementor? It's sort of like that.

What do you picture them wearing? Can you see gestures or hear their voice? Is it large or small? Does it move? And if so, how? For example, does it move gracefully like a ballet dancer, or are its movements rather jerky? Can you dress depression up to seem less daunting? Perhaps put a ridiculous hat on it or put depression in an ugly Christmas sweater? Use a piece of paper to describe and draw depression.

Next, write down your list of difficult thoughts. For example, "I am not good enough," "Life is unfair," or "Things will never get better." These are just examples, so use your own list. Now take

102

your words and place them on the chair. How do you picture them? Do they make noise? Are you able to reach out and touch them? Do they move? If so, how? Write down your observations and notice if that changes how you feel about them.

Do you feel like you have more or less ability about your future choices? With this exercise, you explore your thoughts, and, like the Boggart, you can dress them up so you can find some humor in them. This is not to make light of your depression, but to help you lift them from your shoulders. By taking something scary or depressing and turning it on its head, you can banish your feelings of depression.

Breath Awareness Meditation or Mindful Breathing

Mindfulness meditation focuses on the use of your breath to help train your mind. You can spend only 15 minutes each day focusing on exhaling and inhaling to lessen heightened moods and emotional baggage. It's easy to practice and can be done standing, sitting, or lying down. Your eyes can be open or closed, whichever you prefer.

Using Positive Affirmations

You may not be aware that everything you say and think is an affirmation that molds your thoughts. Negative words and thoughts create negative affirmations, while positive words and thoughts obviously create positive affirmations. This might sound scary, but everything you think and say conditions you to want more of whatever you focus on.

However, this also applies when you say things such as "I no longer want to feel depressed." Unfortunately, our subconscious minds work against us and we only remember the words, feel depressed.

Positive affirmations should become your daily mantra that you repeat every day to retrain your brain toward positive thinking. You may wonder why you need positive mantras, but frankly everyone could use them because our world today is chock-full of negativity. Just five minutes of listening to the media can send us into a spiral of despair, but that is the fault of the world we live in and that is not your responsibility.

Begin your journey toward positivity because unless you commit to making a change, you will be unable to move forward. It's not going to be easy at first and there will be bumps in the road along the way.

You are probably wondering if positive affirmations truly work. Give it a try. After just a few days, you may begin to feel better, but building new habits isn't easy and you have to stick with it.

It can be intimidating to create your own positive affirmations, but there are some things to consider when constructing affirmations that work for you.

Your affirmations must always be in the present tense. So use phrases like I am, or I do and avoid future tenses such as I will, or I am going to.

Only construct your affirmations with positive words like "can," "have," and "do." In order to focus on the positive, your mind needs to hear only positive words.

Keep your affirmations specific regarding what it is that you wish to change. If you want a positive mindset, then your affirmations need to support your goal. Be positive in everything you do, think, and say.

Repetition is the only way that your affirmations will work. Repeat them daily, even following the morning, noon, and nighttime schedule. The more you repeat your affirmations, the more ingrained your new thought processes will become.

Here are a few examples of some positive affirmations so you can format your own.

My life is amazing and fulfilling.

I remain happy and energized every day and put 100% into everything I do.

I have great friends that are there for me.

Pick an area of your life that you want to improve and focus on writing your own positive affirmations. Carpe diem.

Change Your Mindset

Positive affirmations play a part in the goal to change your mindset, but it can be challenging to change your thoughts from negative to positive. The biggest game-changer is mindfulness. And when paired with positive affirmations, self-care, meditation, yoga, and journaling, you can change your thoughts from negative to positive.

We have already explored that mindfulness is the art of being hyper-aware of something. Before you react to a situation or feeling, be mindful and calmly examine all aspects of the situation or feeling and learn to accept it for what it is. Remove any judgment surrounding yourself.

When you find yourself facing a negative thought, take a step back, and instead of reacting, view the thought for what it is, what physical sensations it might produce, and the thoughts that take away your power. By doing so, you will find it easier to release those negative thoughts.

If you focus on the positive, you will find it difficult to be negative. Focusing on the good things in your life will cause less room for negative thoughts. One way you can harness your focus is to keep a gratitude journal so you can remind yourself of all those things around you to be grateful for. By following this practice, healthy thinking will become second nature and become your new healthy habit.

One should never confuse being grateful with just merely giving thanks for the positive things that influence your life. What this means is that you shift your overall perception, allowing you to look deeply into your past and put a different spin on events that may have previously proved painful to you. When you learn to find the good part that dwells inside a bad situation, then you can find that ray of sunshine to grab onto. It is your choice to be thankful and grateful.

Too often people worry about what others think, and when you internalize these thoughts, they can cause issues. By allowing yourself to practice self-acceptance, you can start to view yourself in a positive light. While we all have our bad habits, we can try to improve them without judgment.

Within us all is the power to change the way we think, so when you feel negative thoughts trying to work their way into your mind, break out that gratitude journal, hug your dog, take that walk outside in the sunshine, or even stop and enjoy your favorite brew and quietly reflect. Even the ability to take five will help you distract yourself from the negative.

You may find it a struggle to release your thoughts, but understand that you are not your thoughts. Your thoughts are not a reflection of your soul, goodness, or values, and ultimately you may find that you are spending entirely too much energy fighting your negative thoughts. Following mindfulness, you will be able to achieve your happiness by preventing negative thoughts that wear you down and exhaust your reserves.

It will take constant work on your part to remember to be grateful, practice mindfulness, and be okay with who and what you are. These invaluable tools will aid you in removing barriers and limitations that have kept you from living life to its fullest.

Building Your Focus Through Aromatics

The calming scents of essential oils can help you find focus and calm. Always choose 100% therapeutic oils that have no added chemicals. They may be a bit more expensive, but you don't want to use something harmful. Experiment with whatever scent is right for you. Here are some of the more popular choices.

- Lavender oil can alleviate stress and anxiety while at the same time improving your sleep.
- Frankincense oil brings the sensation of peace and relaxation.
- Rosemary 0il is not just for cooking! This oil may strengthen your memory and relieve pain, which can cause added stress.
- Citrus oils give off a clean crisp scent that can reduce headaches and mental fatigue.
- Peppermint oil can increase your ability to focus by just a single whiff and can relieve headaches and muscle fatigue.

There are many other scents. Choose what calls to you.

The Benefits of Being Active

Imagery isn't the sole solution. Getting some exercise helps boost your energy and your mood. Start small and build from ten to thirty minutes at least a few times each week. We know that depression can inhibit your desire to do much in the way of a workout, but we aren't implying that you join the track team or anything intense. Enjoy the fresh air, sunlight, and walking Fido. Just being around nature can lift your mood. Here's a few ideas, but feel free to add some of your own to the list:

- Biking
- Dance class
- Learn horseback riding
- Hiking
- Jogging
- Skating
- Walking
- Gardening
- Take your dog to agility class
- Yoga

Adding exercise is rewarding, but not always easy and that is why our suggestions are in the "start small" category. You can be creative and make a playlist for when you walk or listen to a comedy routine. Technology may have its downfalls, but it can make exercising more fun! There are plenty of free workout videos to help inspire you. Don't reject the thought of a mindful walk. You can take in nature, let your mind go in the moment and clear the depression cobwebs from the corner of your mind.

Mindful walking is easy, and you only need to be present and noticing what happens within your body and what surrounds your body while you walk. You may find your thoughts wandering, but gently bring them back to your walk.

How about a little yoga to brighten up your day? Yoga can be a fantastic choice to keep your mind and body stronger, happier, and more flexible. You don't have to buy expensive outfits (unless you want to) or even leave the comfort of your own home. Here are a few poses that we recommend. You can do some or all, but always check with your doctor. If you are ever unsure of the poses, you can Google the movements.

- **The cobra.** This movement is meant to change the way you feel and bring your energy level up. Begin by lying facedown on the floor. Your palms should be flat, with your fingers pointed forward, just beneath your shoulders. Spread your fingers apart and press your palms down to enable your torso to lift off the ground. Continue to push your palms down while letting your torso rise. At this point your arms should be as straight as possible. While doing this, keep your feet, legs, and hips on the floor or mat beneath you. Lift and open your chest, while pointing your chin upward and outward. Hold this posture for three or four breaths and as you hold it, take notice of how your body feels. Do you feel a change in your mind or emotional state? Now gently lower yourself back to the floor. You can begin by doing just this exercise alone and gradually transitioning into the next movement.
- **Downward-facing dog.** Begin this pose on your hands and knees, keeping your knees squarely below your hips

and hands beneath your shoulders. Tuck your toes under and shift your weight back while pressing up against your hands. This places your body in an inverted V. See if you can hold this position for 1 to 3 breaths and take care to press all parts of your hands down evenly. Take care not to place all your weight into your wrists. Take notice how you feel in both mind and body. Can you feel your power and strength? Gently lower your knees to the floor and you can follow with the rest of your upper body. Again, if you want to rest or stop, you can always wait until you have built up more muscle memory to add the third and final movement.

- **Upward-facing dog.** Just as in the cobra, this movement opens the chest and stretches out the back. Start facing down on the floor with your hands at your sides, palms on the floor next to your chest. Now, shift your eyes directly in front of you. Inhale, and squeeze your shoulder blades together. Exhale, and press down on your hands, while raising your torso. Pull your shoulder blades back and lift your ribcage. Hold for a few breaths and notice how you feel. Gently lower yourself, and rest lying down.

When you are able to do all three poses, how did they make you feel emotionally or physically? Which exercise felt inspiring?

A Closer Look at Mindfulness

We talked about meditation and mindfulness early on in this book, but can it help you with your depression? If you are hesitant that meditation can help, remember that meditation is more than just thinking positively and putting on a happy face.

We can all agree that depression is filled with dark thoughts. The idea of mindfulness and being in the present moment may sound silly, but being in the present is your chance to let go of the past, forget your worries over your future, and just be you.

You don't have to venture to a mountaintop in the furthest reaches of Tibet and study with monks, or sit lotus style on a cushion in order to practice mindfulness. The beauty is that you can bring mindfulness into every aspect of your daily life. Your life is filled with studying, practicing, walking, activities, eating, and chores. All of these can be done mindfully.

Meditation is all about accepting your thoughts instead of trying to push them out of your mind or pretend that you never had them in the first place. With mindfulness, you notice these thoughts, accept them, and then let them go. This is how meditation can help interrupt your cycles of negative thought. It is not a question of liking an experience you may be having, but mindfulness is just asking you to notice the experience and try not to get in a fight with it. The more you give in to the temptation to clash with something, the more likely it is to hang around and cause more irritation.

The more you are able to stay present in the moment, the easier it will be for you to notice early warning signs of depression. When we talk about acceptance, we are not telling you to just get used to difficult emotions and experiences, or thinking that you need to gain control over a situation. Acceptance is about willingness, and instead of the control you think you need, you will discover that you are willing to face something and follow it through.

The act of mindfulness is not something you practice for a week or two and then you suddenly find everything is better. Mindfulness is not a quick fix and takes time to develop successful habits, but it is a practice that delivers benefits you can continue with throughout your life.

You may feel that meditation is strange, especially if you have never tried it before, but the steps are simple to get started.

There is no right or wrong position from which to meditate. So you can stand up, lie down, or sit down, because it's all just a matter of personal choice. Begin by taking slow, deep breaths through your nose and for the next few moments we are going to ask you to just focus on your breathing. Ask yourself, when was the last time that you sat perfectly still? When was the last time you silenced your phone and put all your distractions away? When was the last time that you sat and did absolutely nothing?

Now focus your attention and describe how it feels to inhale. How does it feel to exhale? What sounds are made with each breath? You may find that your thoughts will wander, but that's a typical response. Just continue to redirect your focus to your breathing whenever this happens. Eventually, you will begin to shift your attention from breathing to a body scan.

Body Scan Meditation

1. Sit or lie comfortably and close your eyes. It is your choice on which position seems more comfortable to you. Take note of what it feels like to be you in this moment.
2. Inhale and exhale deeply. While taking these few deep breaths, describe how your breathing feels within your body.
3. Return your breathing to normal.
4. Begin at your feet, and investigate anything you feel. See if you notice anything like: tingling, warmth, coolness, tension, pressure, or heaviness, etc. Do any of your sensations change while you are in the middle of your observation? How does it change?
5. Let's move on from the focus on your feet and bring awareness to any feelings you might be experiencing in your legs. What do you notice?
6. After you address your legs, move your attention to your back and butt. Are you feeling any pressure or sensations?
7. Next, explore your stomach and chest areas. Can you still feel your breath as it goes in and out? Has it changed from your initial way of breathing? Do you feel your heart beating? Is it steady, or pounding? Are you feeling tense anywhere? Do any areas give you pain? If so, you can add a quick visualization exercise that sends relaxing breaths to the part of your body experiencing pain. Picture the pain easing.
8. Shift your attention now to your hands, arms, and shoulders. Is the air totally still, or can you feel the air

upon your skin? As before, take note of any sensations you might experience.

9. Moving on, you will explore your neck, face, and head regions. Imagine taking notice of these parts of your body for the first time. Can you feel your lips? Your teeth? What do your nose or cheekbones feel like?

10. Finish off your body scan meditation by taking notice of the top of your head. And before you end your session, take a moment to notice your body as a whole lying there. With time and practice, you can expand this meditation and break it down by fingers, toes, ankles, calves, knees, etc.

Remember to make your meditation a habit. Even a small five-minute meditation each day can help you. Try to do this every day at roughly the same time so that you can develop a good habit. It can be as simple as doing a body scan in the shower each morning, or perhaps it's the last thing you do at night before bed. Once you are able to find what works for you, the process will become easier.

There is no "cure" for depression, but there are ways to ease the symptoms. Meditation may be beneficial to add with other therapies. Because depression is very serious, never hesitate to reach out to your parents and healthcare professional.

You have the ability to be responsible for your life. Read the next excerpt to guide you on how.

Five Short Chapters

I

I walk down the street.

There is a deep hole in the sidewalk.

I fall in.

I am lost ... I am helpless.

It isn't my fault.

It takes forever to find a way out.

II

I walk down the same street.

There is a deep hole in the sidewalk.

I pretend I don't see it.

I fall in again.

I can't believe I am in the same place.

But, it isn't my fault.

It still takes a long time to get out.

III

I walk down the same street.

There is a deep hole in the sidewalk.

I see it is there.

I still fall in. It's a habit.

My eyes are open.

I know where I am.

It is my fault. I get out immediately.

IV

I walk down the same street.

There is a deep hole in the sidewalk.

I walk around it.

V

I walk down another street.

Portia Nelson

There's a Hole in My Sidewalk

Exercises & Case Studies

Exercise 1

Let's try a quick visualization exercise!

Close your eyes and allow your mind to revisit an event when you lost track of time. For example, perhaps it was something you did on a vacation that was so amazing that you became completely absorbed. Whatever your event was, go back and revisit it and allow yourself to become immersed in the event. Imagine that it is happening all over again.

Take time to write in your journal about some moments from your past where you have already practiced mindfulness.

STOP is a mindfulness practice from Mitch Abblett, Ph.D (2016).

Stop whatever it is that you are doing at this moment. Put down the phone, your schoolbooks, etc. Just stop moving.

Take a breath. Take the time to really experience the inhale and the exhale.

Observe what's going on. When asked to observe, it means that you observe not only everything going on inside of you, but surrounding you as well.

Proceed. Continue on with whatever you were doing before this exercise.

Exercise 2

In order to break a depression cycle, you need to try and think about things from a different perspective. The ultimate goal is to bring healthier thinking into your life in order to banish negative moods. If you are able to do this on a regular basis, you will find the feelings of depression becoming less intense and they tend not to linger for as long.

- When you are feeling down, take some time to jot down the thoughts that are going through your mind.
- Study them to see if you can replace these negative thoughts with some alternate happier thoughts. Study them, and utilizing self-kindness, consider if you are being fair to yourself.
- Keep a list of those happier thoughts and put that list on your phone, or in your pocket. When you are feeling depressed, take them out and read them.
- Try to do something that your depression prevents you from enjoying. For example, go out to eat with a friend, attend a local event, or have a night out at the movies with friends. Your thoughts, behaviors, and feelings are all tied together so by changing your habits, you can alter your depressed mood.

Case study: Abigail

"I could never remember a time when depression wasn't my constant companion. My parents divorced when I was still very young, so while I could never recall the event, I knew that my father was never there for me. My mother did the best that she could, but it wasn't a very happy childhood.

"As I grew older, I learned that my father had a history of mental illness. I was going to a therapist for my depression and one day

119

during my session, I told her that I wanted to stop blaming my genetic history and try something else. The negatives in my life were dragging me down a dark path and I was exhausted from my daily routine and no friends to call my own.

"She talked a bit about mindfulness, but I didn't really understand what it was all about. We decided to give it a try to see if it could produce the effect I was looking for. A calm, happy mind. I was debilitated from all the depression I carried. I wanted freedom for my mind and soul.

"My therapist handed me a pre-recorded guided meditation and I took it home and tried it that night before bedtime. I recall that at first when I was lying in bed, I thought this whole idea was ridiculous. But I breathed a big disgusted sigh and decided to give it a chance.

"I can still recall the imagery. The soft, calm voice told me to imagine I was sitting on a large hill that overlooked a stream that flowed down the side of a mountain and out through a flowery meadow. At the far end of the meadow stood a deep and ancient forest. All through the recording, I was told to take a breath and imagine the colors, the sounds, and the smells of nature all around me.

"Floating down the stream were some dried-up leaves that were headed for the forest. I was told to take all my negative thoughts and place them upon the leaves passing by. Then all I could do was watch my troubles drift away and disappear.

"At first I didn't notice much of a difference, but I was determined to give this mindfulness thing a try. After several weeks, I began to notice that my mind was more calm. For the first time in sixteen years, I think I finally smiled. I have a long road ahead of me, but I am finally able to see some light at the end of a very dark tunnel."

Chapter 5: ADHD

"Yoga introduced me to a style of meditation. The only meditation I would have done before would be in the writing of songs." – Sting, musician

If you are a typical teen, you already have a long laundry list of demands, but if you are a teen with ADHD, you are probably aware that you are going to have to try twice as hard to meet those same requirements. You will probably feel frustrated, exhausted, and stressed-out at times, but don't give up. There are some great resources out there to help you along your path.

Teens with ADHD worry that they will have difficulties focusing their attention long enough to calm their minds and bodies. There are exercises out there that are shorter in length, and with practice, one can find their ability to process them becoming easier and easier.

Remember to keep to small steps and increase times as you become more comfortable with your new skills.

ADHD stands for attention deficit hyperactivity disorder. According to the American Psychiatric Association (2020), ADHD is the most common medical disorder affecting children and teens today. If you have an inability to focus, can't seem to hold still, or make hurried actions without thinking things through, you could be suffering from ADHD.

The APA (2020) went on to say that over eight percent of children and over 2 percent of adults suffer from ADHD, and it is more common in males than females.

ADHD is diagnosed as three different types based upon symptoms, which are observed over the course of around 6 months. The following symptoms are displayed frequently.

Inattentive Type

- Makes careless mistakes or doesn't pay close attention to detail
- Cannot stay focused on tasks or activities
- Unable to listen and has their attention drift when being spoken to
- Does not follow through when given instructions. They may begin a task, but lose focus and do not finish.
- Has difficulties organizing tasks/work, therefore misses deadlines, cannot manage time well and can have unorganized work ethic
- Avoids tasks that require mental prowess or completing forms
- Frequently loses items needed for daily life, such as books, keys, cell phone, or eyeglasses
- Becomes easily distracted
- Forgets daily chores

Hyperactive Impulse Type

- Has an inability to sit still and fidgets with hands or feet
- Will not be able to stay seated in restaurants, classrooms, etc.
- When inappropriate, will run around or climb
- Appear to always be on the go and inexhaustible
- Talk incessantly
- Will not wait for a question to be finished and blurt out an answer
- Shows an inability to wait for their turn in a conversation or while waiting in line for something
- May step in and take over what others are doing

Combined Type

The combined type will have symptoms from both of the other kinds of ADHD.

Are you a teen suffering from ADHD? It's difficult enough to keep up grades, prepare for the advancement into adulthood, and attend college, but what if you have an added difficulty?

Teens with ADHD often have to work twice as hard to keep their focus at school. Though some symptoms differ from individual to individual, many experience a lack of focus and concentration, forgetfulness, poor decision-making, hyperactivity, and heightened emotions. Teens with ADHD might feel like adrenaline junkies and frequently have a myriad of ideas swirling around in their brains like a Category 5 tornado. They might seek out stress and drama. The thought of meditating might just make them scream into a pillow. That said, the good news is that meditation can help stabilize the symptoms of ADHD. The bad news is that it can be difficult to persuade a teen with ADHD to give meditation a try.

Don't worry, we have a few tips that will make this a user-friendly experience. You do not have to sit in the lotus position to practice meditation; in fact, you don't have to sit down at all! It is not required that you have a mantra or practice yoga. It is very difficult—nay, impossible—to fail at meditation, as it is easily adjusted to suit every personality.

If you have a racing brain, try these steps:

- Repeat as often as necessary, even if it's a million times, "Meditation is achieved by practice. I plan to learn from this experience. There are no wrong ways to meditate."
- Be comfortable. There's no such thing as too comfortable. If you fall asleep, you most likely need it!
- Find your comfort zone. Being comfortable while meditating is crucial. You are going to be the best judge of what works for you. Whether it is lying on your bed, walking at a slow pace up and down the hallway, or sitting on a swing from a large oak tree in the backyard— just do it.
- Take slow and even breaths. Practice relaxing and let your breath flow naturally.
- It is going to be a challenge to train your brain to switch gears quickly to settle down into a meditation mode.

Perhaps construct a premeditation rite of taking a hot bath or shower, putting on comfortable clothing, and listening to soothing music before you meditate. This will lessen the shock of changing states and ensure a smooth transition for mind and body into meditation.

- Sensory cues. You may find that certain sensory cues help you move from one mental state to another. Perhaps you have a very soft, comfortable shirt that you can now designate as your meditation shirt. You may enjoy using a diffuser with lavender, or perhaps you enjoy the sound of a light rain falling in a tropical rainforest. This is your meditation time, you get to choose what works best for you. Instrumental music is usually best. Skip the lyrics, because the words can be distracting and break your intention.

- Choose your focus. Your focus may be a guided recording. Some can simply focus on breathing, while others repeat a word or phrase in their minds (mantra). If it's the holiday season, you might enjoy sitting quietly by the Christmas tree and gazing at the ornaments and lights.

- A moving meditation is just as suitable as sitting. Don't try to force what you consider a "should" when meditating. Sometimes, for the active ADHD teen, meditation is most productive through a simple, quiet, distraction-free walk.

- Stick with it. Especially when you begin your path down meditation lane, it's likely that you will have to bring your mind back to focus often. Don't get frustrated. As you now know, meditation becomes easier and easier with repetition.

- Keep your sessions short at first. It's unreasonable to meditate for twenty minutes for your first meditation experience. When you become more comfortable in your meditation routine, feel free to increase the length as your sessions become more relaxed and comforting. When this happens, you are experiencing some of meditation's benefits.
- Keep a routine. If you have ADHD or have trouble sticking with a routine, it can be as simple as setting an alarm for the same time each day, reminding you to breathe. If you are really struggling, there are coaches specialized in ADHD to help keep you on track.
- Change your brain with Transcendental Meditation. There have been some recent studies suggesting that Transcendental Meditation reduces some of the symptoms of ADHD. According to TM® for women (2013), there have been results pointing to the use of Transcendental Meditation and changes within the brain. Brainwave patterns—especially the ratio between beta and theta waves—have links to ADHD severity. TM practice appears to delay development of certain frontal brain changes which lessen ADHD symptoms.

Presently, there are no known specific causes of ADHD. Thus far, there is unsupported evidence that it could be genetic or random stresses during pregnancy. At this time, doctors and researchers are not sure of the causes surrounding the development of ADHD. What others need to understand is that sufferers of ADHD aren't lazy, it is a developmental disorder of the brain. If you are concerned that you have ADHD, you should talk to your health care professional and determine what is going on in your life.

If you have ADHD, you can help yourself immensely by eating healthy foods, getting proper rest/sleep, being active with some form of exercise, and practicing mindfulness and breathing exercises.

If someone suffers from ADHD, they may have difficulties focusing enough to get their schoolwork done. The problem is ADHD teens crave a lot of stimulation and excitement, so writing a paper on the fall of the Roman Empire can take them a long time to complete. Parents and teachers sometimes don't realize that ADHD students do not learn from the punishment/rewards system like other pupils.

What's it like for teens with ADHD? When you experience the effects of ADHD, you can feel overwhelmed, chaotic, and out of control. It's not that you don't want to write that paper, but the overpowering enormity of the organization to write such a piece can make you want to run around the house dispensing a case of silly string along the way. You may often feel bad about yourself because you get rebuked for things you can't help, like not listening, losing your temper, or performing tasks too quickly and making mistakes. Just know that ADHD and their afflictions are not your fault and you have nothing to feel badly about.

There are some common myths surrounding ADHD. The first one is that teens are hyperactive. Parents may not realize that by the time their child has reached the teenage years, hyperactivity has usually been replaced with restlessness. Secondly, it is generally believed that teens with ADHD cannot sit still for ten minutes. Despite the misinformation out there, teenage students can and do sit still in class. However, they may daydream or fall asleep. Myth three is that ADHD disappears in teens and adults. Originally it was believed that people outgrow ADHD because

128

of their hyperactivity decreasing. There is currently no science proving that ADHD can be outgrown, but the use of meditation can engage the brain of an ADHD sufferer. In regards to minimizing the symptoms of ADHD, mindfulness meditation shows the most promise. Guided meditation apps and videos (see our section on There's an App for That), can be effective for a brain that needs engagement over more traditional methods. Generally, people believe that ADHD is overdiagnosed. Because of more research being done, the diagnosis has really just caught up since ADHD had truly been underdiagnosed for years.

While ADHD can make it difficult to ignore pesky distractions, which lead you astray, it can also make you concentrate so intensely that you can work at a project for hours and not realize how much time has flown by. This mode is referred to as hyperfocus. The only downside to hyperfocus is that you can get caught up in your tunnel vision, which can get in the way of the rest of your life. For example, you want to just check one little fact out on the internet regarding your paper on the Roman Empire, then suddenly several hours have ticked by and you have wasted hours online that might make you late in your pre-sleep wind-down, miss your date with the cute girl in chemistry class, or late for your after-school job. This can put a strain on relationships, schoolwork, and your health. But if you can get a handle on your hyperfocus, it could turn into your biggest asset.

How does one meditate for ADHD? The brain of someone with ADHD can make them feel like an adrenaline junkie, purposely looking for stress and drama because they thrive on it. Teens that suffer from ADHD do not have to sit down to meditate, stop moving, or develop a mantra if those practices make them uncomfortable. What you do have to keep in mind is utilizing meditation to counteract all the bad habits you have developed while your ADHD had control.

- Meditation takes time. Try not to overload your brain by forcing lengthy sessions which can be a turn-off. Begin with a time as short as two minutes and increase when you feel comfortable doing so.
- If your schedule allows, set your meditation for first thing in the morning.
- There are no set rules to meditation, so you are able to do what works best for you. If being inside gives you unease, take your meditation to the great outdoors.
- Stay calm and give meditation a chance to work for you. Even if you don't realize it, everyone needs a little relaxation.

Unfortunately, you cannot just turn your ADHD traits on and off like a light switch, but you can become more in tune with what causes you to focus in on certain things. As an example, you are most likely to lose yourself in activities that you find interesting, while others you just mentally wander away from.

Keep records of things that snag your attention and, in addition, a list of things that turn you away. Can you spend an entire day doing a puzzle, but when it comes to Geometry you can only look at it for a few seconds before going off in another direction?

We know that being hyperfocused can make you lose time, so in order to avoid missing your needed sleep, avoid engaging in triggers before bedtime or before set times that you need to be at school, work, or out with friends.

If you suspect that you have gotten caught up in your hyperfocus, even though you may find it hard, you must redirect your focus. So if Spot is waiting at the front door, clip on his leash and take him for a walk, do a couple of deep breathing exercises, or empty/load the dishwasher. A change of venue will prove helpful.

Decide how much time you want to dedicate to work on a task. Let's say you come home from school and you want to work on that fall of the Roman Empire paper. But because you get engrossed in the internet, you want to devote only two hours each night this week immediately after you get home from classes. Set an alarm on your phone to go off when you need to break away from this project because you have other plans. It usually takes the brain a few extra minutes to shift gears, so build in a fifteen-minute buffer between tasks.

Cutting off distractions ahead of time will help you get the most out of your time. Make a list of everything you are going to need for your project, and before you sit down to begin, gather them all together so you will not need to stop and look for a missing piece. Also, during this time, tone down the digital distractions. Turn off your phone notifications and keep your phone out of reach to avoid temptations.

While you will not always be able to control the things that pull you away from your destination, you can help yourself by including a step-by-step process of the steps you need to reach in the attainment of your goal. You may choose to include some regular timeouts to help you break the enchantment of hyperfocus. Every forty-five minutes or so, get up and do something else for a few minutes. You can read a chapter in a book or vacuum your room. The timeout itself is not important, so long as it is not another task that you typically hyperfocus on.

You can manage it by breaking the project up into smaller pieces, which will not send you over the edge. With this simple method, you can prioritize tasks, keep instructions and information at your fingertips, and be able to complete your task.

Can you have ADHD and not appear to be hyper? Absolutely. The inattentive type (see above), has trouble paying attention and is prone to make careless mistakes, lose things, and demonstrate an inability to follow through.

Are there any positives involved with ADHD? Honestly, according to Smitha Bhandari, MD (2019), students with ADHD scored better on tests, had very high creativity scores, and were proficient in drama, music, visual arts, and scientific discoveries. A German study also found that being impulsive gave the ADHD subject an ability to hyperfocus and their impulsive tendencies made them great entrepreneurs.

There are some people out there you may not be aware of who suffer from ADHD: U.S. Olympic champion Simone Biles, Olympic champion Michael Phelps, Justin Timberlake, Super Bowl champion Terry Bradshaw, and even Paris Hilton. All of them have gone on to have some astonishingly jaw-dropping careers. So there is nothing stopping you from your own personal success.

Exercise and Case Study

Case Study: Kevin

"I had a very difficult time through junior high and high school. My parent-teacher conferences were all very heated and I was always described as lazy. The teachers I had really didn't understand me and they certainly made no effort to figure out why I couldn't pay attention in class and sometimes fell asleep. I was described as not bothering to listen in class or realize I had been called upon to answer a question in front of the class.

"I admit I probably did appear lazy, but I was easily distracted and often angry about it. It wasn't that I didn't want to do my essays. I would come home with the best intentions and after a few minutes of looking things up on the internet, I would get distracted, and before I knew it, it was bedtime. My student years were filled with unfinished projects and incomplete grades. I was really in danger of being held back a year and I really didn't want that, so I became more depressed.

"I became hounded at home with negative reinforcement because my parents didn't understand. Why should they? I didn't understand it myself.

"One day my regular teacher wasn't in class and we had a substitute teacher. She noticed my inability to stay focused and pay attention to detail and she knew right away that I had ADHD. Miss Kinzie took the time to show up to my next parent-teacher conference and had a talk with both my parents and my regular teacher.

"After explaining all the signs that they had missed, and that I was not, in fact, lazy, she made some recommendations about activities that I could do to help build my skills. Miss Kinzie suggested that I could add in some mindfulness meditation techniques along with a few yoga movements to try and rewire the way I thought.

"I was game, because the last thing I wanted was to be held back a year. Something else changed in me that day also. Miss Kinzie, a teacher but a complete stranger, had believed in me when no one else had. The impact that she had on my life was astonishing. All this time I felt like I was going crazy. Someone had helped me just in time because I was ready to give up.

"Giving me the benefit of the doubt, I was passed into the next grade level, giving me an entire summer of working with a yoga instructor that had credentials in dealing with ADHD teens. I worked very hard before school started again and I felt more confident and had tools at my disposal to help me deal with my distractions. There were no more unfinished assignments and no more punishment was doled out. I finally felt understood. Now as I come close to ending my final year in high school, I already have a professional goal in life and have been accepted at three of my top pick colleges. I feel renewed and confident. All because of one educator who noticed that I wasn't really lazy after all. I feel sure that Miss Kinzie has gone on to help a lot of students like myself."

Exercise

What can I do to help me study best at home? Break out paper and pencil and let's figure out what works best for you when you want to study at home. Write down anything that you feel applies to you.

- When is the best time for you to study?
  - When I first get home from school.
  - After school, but I need a quick break before I get started.
  - Start right after dinner.
  - In the morning before I go to school?
- With whom can I study best?
  - Alone.
  - When someone else is present in the room.
  - A friend.
  - A parent.
  - A tutor.
- Where do I feel I can study the best?
  - In my bedroom.
  - Just on the floor, no specific room.
  - On my bed.
  - At my desk.
  - At the kitchen table.
  - In a chair in the family room.
- Do I need anything else while I study?
  - Do I need to be sitting?
  - Do I study better lying down?
  - Does it need to be super quiet?
  - Do I need a desk lamp?
  - Do I work well with some quiet music playing in the background?
- What is the optimum time I can study before I need a break?
  - Fifteen minutes.
  - Thirty minutes.

- An hour.
- What can I do to help me complete my homework and stay organized?
  - Use a planner to help me keep track of my assignments and due dates.
  - Call a friend for the assignments.
  - Keep extra copies of my books at home.
  - Plan what I do first.
  - Figure out how long each step of the assignment will take.
  - Put my finished work in one place.
  - Color code my book covers and folders.
- What tools can I use to help me learn/remember information?
  - Write things down.
  - Draw a picture to help me remember.
  - Use flash cards.
  - Type information into my computer.
  - Listen to a recording I have made regarding the information needed.
  - Read aloud.

If you come up with different ideas, make sure to jot down what helps you.

Remember To Be Silly

Laughter and acting silly can relieve stress and create a contented mindset. Even if you aren't truly happy, pretending that you are can still end up putting a smile on your face. Acting happy can actually make you feel better about yourself. You can always remind yourself to be silly by sticking a post-it on your bathroom mirror.

1. Sing and dance in the rain and even stomp through some big puddles and splash about.
2. Explore laughter yoga. This is a great combination of yoga, deep breathing exercises, and laughter exercises. This technique will strengthen the immune system and

reduce your stress. Laughter will help to create a positive mental state and provide hope during tough times. Laughter is the best medicine!

3. Have a contest with your friends, for example, try to see which one of you can stuff the greatest amount of marshmallows in your mouth.

Meditation

So what is mindfulness, and how is it going to help? Mindfulness can happen naturally, but it means to pay attention to something and really notice what you are doing without distractions. For example, let's say that you are riding your horse on a jumping course. There is a pattern involved in your course that you must follow, but you also need to ride each fence individually and may have to make last-minute adjustments on the approach. The ability to tune out everything else and concentrate on the job at hand is the very epitome of mindfulness.

When you have a weak muscle, you need to perform exercises to strengthen it, and mindfulness is the exercise you practice in order to build up your brain's muscles.

If you are worried that mindfulness is just religious mumbo jumbo, let us assure you that it is not. Even though the roots of meditation and mindfulness might have emanated from religion, it really just involves paying close attention to your feelings, thoughts, and bodily sensations. In other words, it entails what is happening to you right now in this moment. Mindfulness can be used to assist you in a plethora of wellness techniques.

You may be asking why you need mindfulness, but there are some skills you need that it will help you attain.

- Allows you to pay attention better and listen to others
- Permits you to learn more
- Learn to be less distracted
- Helps you to gain self-control and avoid becoming easily upset
- Enables you to feel happier, thus get more enjoyment out of things
- Allows you to become more patient
- Helps program you to slow down instead of always rushing
- Stay calm when under stressful situations
- Stop procrastinating and get tasks finished

The skills that mindfulness teaches can improve everyone, especially those who suffer from ADHD. They help you to become calmer and enhance your focus when you have a difficult task ahead.

Practicing mindfulness can help you gain skills and rewire your brain so that you no longer struggle. You will be able to improve your concentration, organization skills, and motivate yourself. Mindfulness will also improve your ability to self-observe and control your attention.

We know that you are most likely skeptical. You are probably thinking, well, alrighty then, just a few minutes each day and my ADHD will go bye-bye. Well, not exactly. Sure, your meditation sessions are going to play an important role, and mindfulness will be used throughout each day, but these are tactics for the long haul. You will learn to apply mindfulness on your own by just sitting down in a comfortable place where you won't be disturbed. You can begin by spending just five minutes focusing on the sensation of breathing in and breathing out. Pay close attention to what it feels like when your stomach rises and falls. Do this every day and after a few weeks, you can increase your time up to twenty minutes or more. You can slip this in before tests, in advance of being the next in line to bat in gym class, or before meeting your friends for a social event that is giving you a bit of anxiety. The great thing is, no one will ever know you are doing it. Remember too that mindfulness can be done sitting or walking, so there are no telltale signs that you even practice it.

You are just beginning your journey to mindfulness meditation for your ADHD, so don't be discouraged if this process takes you a few months to start seeing real results.

Are you ready to change yourself for the better and succeed? Great, let's get started!

More than likely your ADHD isn't always a problem because you probably experience times when it seems better than others. For example, you may find that while participating in your favorite sport where you get to move your body constantly, it is much easier for you than sitting through math class. Let's see if we can't nail down when and where your ADHD symptoms cause you the most difficulties. Write down your answers to these questions.

- What do you feel is the most severe symptom you experience with your ADHD?
- Write down any situations that you have experienced that exacerbate your symptoms.
- Are there situations that make this symptom better?

- During the situations that cause your ADHD to be more severe, are there any changes you could make to minimize your symptoms?
- Is there something you could change in your environment to change your symptoms for the better?
- It can be difficult to experience these difficulties and you might feel that others have it easy compared to you. Think of a person that represents this and think about challenges that they may be facing.
- Everyone is a unique individual, including you! Can you think of some talents or skills that make you an amazingly unique person?

Yoga for ADHD

So, you are on board with mindfulness meditation and you are wondering about yoga. What a great choice, because yoga is all about slowing down and focusing! According to CHADD (2020), researchers are finding that the practice of yoga can have positive effects on children and teens who have been diagnosed with ADHD—effects that last after they leave the yoga mat for the day. These studies went on to find that when done approximately two times a week, yoga can help decrease some of the symptoms suffered with ADHD. Most noticeably was the difference in being able to pay attention in class and an improvement in classroom skills. So yoga, in conjunction with mindfulness, can make a difference to teens with ADHD.

There is no special equipment to buy. If you want one, a yoga mat is great. Other than that, all you need is comfortable clothes and a quiet place. Or if you prefer to be in a group, you can find a yoga class to participate in. You are able to find free resources online that provide you with exercises aimed at specific age groups.

CHADD's study (2020), also showed that if a parent and child practice yoga at the same time, they are more likely to strengthen each other's new habit.

Also according to CHADD (2020), they reported that yoga has been shown to help improve ADHD symptoms. Practicing yoga moves for twenty minutes twice a week for 8 weeks improved the subject's testing that measured attention and focus.

During your introduction to yoga, you may experience different emotions and energy levels. For example, you could feel supercharged with electricity. While practicing yoga, you will focus on your breathing much like your mindfulness exercises. In yoga however, you will be learning how to inhale or exhale during executions of movements within a pose.

Yoga has other benefits too. It can help boost your self-esteem, lower your stress, and even help you to lose weight. Let's look at some yoga poses that are good for relaxing and drawing out excess energy. (You can also look back to Chapter 4 for some additional poses.)

- **Tree pose.** The tree pose is an excellent choice for working on focus and concentration because you must remain balanced while focusing. Begin by standing with your palms together in front of your sternum as if you were praying. While keeping your palms together and inhaling slowly raise your palm position and arms up over your head. Now exhale slowly and bring your arms back into their original position. Repeat this several times so that you can work on your coordination between breaths and movement. When you have mastered this, you are ready to add in the balancing part of this exercise. Start by focusing on an unmoving spot on the floor in front of you. Raise your left leg and place your left foot up against your right calf. Hold this pose for five breaths, then release and switch to the other side and do the same.

- **The cat-cow pose.** For this yoga exercise, begin by getting on your hands and knees. You will want to keep your knees in line with your hips. Keep your wrists, elbows, and shoulders perpendicular to the floor. Begin your inhale and slowly round your spine in the direction of the ceiling. When you raise your back, your head will lower, giving the silhouette of a startled cat. Hold that pose for a single second. Now exhale, and return your body to its original starting position. The next inhale, you will lift your head, chest, and tailbone toward the ceiling, causing your back to curve down. You will also hold this pose for a single second and then return your body back to the original position. Exhale. Repeat these positions up to ten times.

- **The seated forward bend.** Begin in a seated position, extending your legs in front of you. Sit tall using good posture. When you inhale, lift your arms overhead, and then exhale folding forward and reaching for your toes. Hold in position for ten seconds, and then return to your starting position. Repeat up to ten times.

- **The seated twist.** To begin, sit comfortably in a cross-legged position. Inhale, then exhale placing your right hand on your left knee. Placing your left hand behind your tailbone, gently twist your torso to the left while looking over your left shoulder. Hold that position for ten seconds, then return to your starting position. Repeat this movement in the opposite direction. You can also do this set up to ten times.
- **The roaring lion.** Lion's breath or simhasana (sim-has-anna). This has been named lion's breath, because your position resembles the pose of a lion. It is preferred to do this practice in the morning, but it can be done in the evening as long as you have 4 to 6 hours between your meal and this practice. This is a basic yoga movement that strengthens your throat, voice, and lungs. The lion pose is said to have some fantastic benefits, like reducing stress and tension, ridding infections in your respiratory tract, and curing stuttering, teeth grinding, and back pain. This is meant to be a fun exercise to keep you rejuvenated. Take position on the floor by kneeling and crossing your ankles so that the front of the right ankle crosses over the back of the left ankle. Your feet must be pointing out on both sides. Place your hand palms down on your knees and spread your fingers apart while pressing them firmly into your knees. While you inhale through your nose, open your mouth while stretching out your tongue. Curl the tip of your tongue toward your chin. Your eyes should be wide open for this and you should feel the muscles in the front of your throat contract. Exhale through your mouth while producing a "ha" sound. In order to perform this correctly, your

breath should pass over the back of the throat. Roar a few times lion style, then change the orientation of your ankle cross to the opposite position and repeat.

- **The wide-knee child's pose.** This is a resting pose that provides a sense of calm. Anyone having knee or hip injuries should sit this one out. Kneel on your floor, bringing your big toes together. Hold your knees a hips-width apart, while you exhale and lay your body onto your thighs. Your hands should rest beside you, pointing to the back of the room with your palms facing up. Doing this should release any shoulder tension. Your forehead should be on the ground and while in this position, gently roll your head from side to side. Breathe slow and steady.

Use your creativity and design your own yoga routine. Having a deep breathing/yoga session once a day is a good start to a new you. The more you practice, the more quickly you become integrated in your new routine and the more comfortable you will become with the exercises. Don't set your expectation bar too high. It may take some time for helpful changes to happen, so don't get discouraged. You are so brave for trying new things!

By watching videos online, you can take a look at these poses if you have any questions on how to execute them.

If you decide to look for a yoga class in your area, be sure to talk with the teachers involved, because not all of them have the experience involved in working with someone with ADHD.

Chapter 6: Meditation for Guided Healing

"Meditation brings wisdom; lack of meditation leaves ignorance. Know well what leads you forward and what holds you back, and choose the path that leads to wisdom." – Buddha

Millions of people live with chronic pain and, surprisingly, there are many teens like yourself that are represented within these numbers. Your family may not understand your withdrawal. It could be that you are having severe mood swings, but now is not the time to become secretive about what you are experiencing.

If you are experiencing any chronic pain, you should talk with your parents and healthcare provider about them immediately. Teens will tend to differ on how they choose to convey that they are experiencing pain within their bodies. The best way is to just be forthcoming about your pain directly and pinpoint exactly where you are experiencing your pain. Talk with your parents about it so they understand what you are going through and can act accordingly.

You may not even realize how you are affected by your pain, so please be aware of yourself and your actions. Emotional signs of pain can include quick mood swings, such as:

- Irritability
- Anger
- Frustration
- Anxiety

- Sadness
- Silence
- Sensitivity

In addition to the emotional signs, you may find that you are exuding behavioral signs as well. Please be aware if you are experiencing any of the following:

- A reduction in sports participation
- Feeling a need to be secretive
- A partial or complete withdrawal from normal school or social activities
- Avoiding situations that may produce pain
- The act of regression, where you ask for help dressing, or want to sleep with a parent, like you would do when you were younger
- Sealing yourself off from others by spending more time alone in a bedroom
- Experiencing changes in appetite
- The sudden desire to sleep or rest more than normal
- An increase in substance abuse
- Performing acts of self-harm

Keep a helpful list of issues surrounding your chronic pain. It will be helpful to know how much your everyday tasks are affected by it or if it is affecting your sleep. By keeping a detailed account of your issues, you will be better able to communicate them to your parents.

There needs to be a better understanding in the treatment of chronic pain issues. Medical providers often look for the nearest Band-Aid, while addressing these complaints, but drugs and opioids have proven not to be the best option. There are numerous teens that worry about the risk of prescription misuse. Truthfully, there is a lot of concern out there that the medications are as big a detriment to your life as the chronic pain, perhaps even more.

Chronic pain can be very complex and merits a more complex treatment approach than just a bottle of often ineffective pills that merely addresses symptoms. Access to treatments that are non-pharmacological can be difficult to find, but they are out there and available. These techniques will keep you at a functioning level while you reset your brain to deal with the chronic pain.

Dealing with the pain from a specific injury is not the same as the experiences of chronic pain. That would be acute pain, which is the sensing of tissue damage by your nerves. This is a simple puzzle where your body gets injured and you hurt, for example you fall down and twist your ankle. Some rest, elevation, ice, and ibuprofen will pretty much zap you back to your old self in no time.

Chronic pain, however, is not the same kind of pain that you experience from an injury. It can begin with an injury or tissue damage, but becomes prolonged well after the initial injury would have healed. According to a Yale University study authored by Chadi Abdallah (2017), studies have concluded that the persistent pain is created by additional stress, environmental effects, and emotional effects, which add to the intensity and continued experience of pain. Chronic pain is defined as a pain that has been consistent for 3 months or more. Sometimes, the root cause of the chronic pain is not apparent, but it typically starts with an injury or diagnosis of disease.

Mental muscle can use its processes to alter the individual's sensory phenomena and that includes the pain. You have seen examples where athletes suffer an injury but can continue to play in their competitions. Because scientists have been expanding their knowledge of the nervous system and how it can work, they have over the last decade focused their attention on how meditation works.

According to Abdallah, researchers have concentrated their attention concerning meditation's effects on the regulation of body awareness, depression, addiction, and PTSD. The studied application of meditation has been shown to reduce pain, often significantly.

Does meditation help? If so, how?

Meditation is proven to impact cognitive functions and increase changes within different regions of the brain. Not only affecting learning, memory, and emotion centers within the brain, meditation can use brain pathways to make changes in how we deal with pain. By using meditation to "call the shots," so to speak, your brain can actually restructure itself to make you less pain-sensitive. While the research regarding meditation and the effects it has on relief of chronic pain is ongoing, there have been some promising studies done supporting meditation's ability to create changes within both brain and body that significantly reduce chronic pain.

Great, but why is meditation effective?

Your body creates this vicious, never-ending circle when you experience chronic pain. So, here you are stressed and in pain, you struggle to maintain your composure while the pain shoots through you like lightning, but you can't figure out why the pain just never stops. This trigger of pain causes stress to the body, which triggers the release of stress hormones. Your brain registers this and sends a response of fight or flight, which causes increased pain and inflammation to race to your already irritated areas, reinforcing the pain. Meditation introduces a calmness to your mind, which signals the body to slow down. When you can settle your brain, it ceases to continually release those stress hormones into your bloodstream and your pain will decrease. In effect, your brain must "unlearn" pain.

Through meditation, your brain is able to release a natural pain reliever, called endorphins. As your brain relaxes, it encourages your muscles and tissues in and around your joints to "settle down." Meditation therefore helps your mind to shift away from your pain.

Although several recent studies have been performed with very promising results, please keep in mind that each individual is different, and just as not every meditation works for everyone, meditation may have diverse results in the amount of pain reduction it can affect.

Relief of Chronic Pain

"I was just fourteen at the time and can still remember the sharp stabbing pain that radiated through my back as if it were yesterday. I had fallen and tumbled out of control down the family stairs until I hit the ground at the base. I had landed in an unceremonious heap and could hear an audible crack when I hit the ground floor. In that moment my life took a huge detour. I just lay there thinking I had certainly broken my back.

"We all thought I had been lucky, because the doctors had found no breaks or signs of fracturing. However, within just one year, I began to experience severe headaches and joint pain. Chronic pain had settled in and had become an unwanted part of my life.

"Just short of two years after the initial accident, the pain became so intense that I could barely hold my school books, climb the stairs to my bedroom, or

help with household chores, and I had to forego the thought of driver's education.

"My days were filled with tears, depression, and drugs. I could see that I would only get progressively worse and doubted that I would be able to have much of a life. Grasping at straws, my mother took me to see Dr. Warren, who instead of more pain killers, suggested that I try meditation.

"Mom and I tried it together. I think she wanted me to know that I wasn't facing this alone. I honestly had no hope of it helping me, but I was pleasantly surprised when I found that it did exactly that.

"While sitting through my guided meditations, I took notice of my breath and body sensations. I swear that I could actually feel the deep knots of pain loosen and relax. I finally had hope.

"Now a year later, I am seventeen, and while I still get the occasional headache or other chronic pain issues, my encounters have dramatically changed. When I experience the occasional flare-up, I know that there is something that can be done about it." – Sophia 17, UT

The most common types of chronic pain are:

- Low back pain
- Migraine and other headache pain
- Neck and facial pain
- Post-trauma pain
- Postsurgical pain
- Arthritis pain
- Neurogenic pain (pain caused by nerve damage
- Chronic fatigue syndrome
- Endometriosis
- Fibromyalgia

Anyone enduring chronic pain on a daily basis can tell you how important it is to get control of the situation. Chronic illness can be confusing, can drain your life force, and can ruin your life if you allow it. What everyone is looking for is the healthiest way to minimize their pain and control it.

The management of pain often needs to push beyond the boundaries of physical and psychological support. That promising treatment is called mindfulness meditation. The goal of this option is to help the subject gain control over his or her pain. We recently described chronic pain; mindfulness helps you to understand the different types of pain and, in effect, control them, to turn down the pain receptors within. When you are able to tap into any extra anxiety, stress, and or depression that you have come to associate with your pain, mindfulness can assist you in relaxing and allowing your body to take over and begin the healing process.

In a paper by Danny Penman, Ph.D. (2015), he cites that there have been clinical trials performed on mindful meditation and the effects they have had on chronic pain. Across the board, over fifty percent was the average reduction, and those practiced in meditation were able to achieve a whopping ninety percent. Meditation has a long history of being suggested as a way to help with medical conditions, and each year the research expands. While you should always talk these treatments over with your parents and health care providers, this could prove to be just what you are looking for to manage your pain relief symptoms.

Let's begin by addressing your greatest fear about the use of meditation to combat chronic pain. One of the huge deterrents that people experience, when they think of using meditation, is that they fear they will discover that the pain is really all in their heads after all.

These are understandable concerns, especially when you are discovering new territory yourself, but just because meditation uses our mind, doesn't mean that you have created the pain to issue from there in the first place.

Meditation has been used by people recovering from surgery to help them deal with their postoperative pain. No one would be able to accuse them of having their mind make that pain up. Coincidentally, research from Wake Forest School of Medicine was quoted by the *Hindustan Times* (2018) stating that there have been studies that show that people who meditate have higher pain thresholds than people who do not practice meditation.

When we experience chronic pain, we will do anything to distract ourselves from the constant thought of giving it more attention. Before meditation became a viable option, people were instructed to find distractions to take their mind off the constant focus, however, that never really seemed to work because the brain remained aware of the pain and it never dealt with it. Surprisingly, mindfulness meditations encourage you to use the opposite approach. These meditations typically urge you to give in to your attention and counsel you to be more aware, rather than becoming sidetracked. In other words, you are not trying to block the pain, but embrace it and work with it.

However, just giving in to your attention isn't all that matters, it also has to do with the quality of awareness that you assign to the chronic pain you have been experiencing. People with chronic pain can create a sense of hyper-awareness, giving them extra sensitivity to their pain. Unfortunately, this isn't productive in the reduction of pain, and it may even make it worse for the sufferer. Meditation creates a practice that is focused.

By focused, we mean that our attention only gets directed to where we tell it to go. Meditation teaches us to attend to our minds in a fashion that helps us to reduce our suffering. The ability to learn how to focus our attention on our pain is the mindfulness strategy. The more we practice, the more we can become aware of our responses and can learn to regulate them to help us manage our pain.

How, you ask? Begin by tuning into your pain and ask yourself the following question. What else do I experience in my body when I feel this pain? What you are using this question for is to point your attention toward the reaction you have when you experience the pain.

Often your answer may be an obvious one. For instance, you may experience a flood of worried thoughts or a feeling of familiarity. No one wants to be in pain, but having become accustomed to it, you may feel afraid to be without it. It is similar to when we have an injury, say a twisted ankle, and we walk a bit differently to accommodate that injury. We find that even after it has healed we continue to walk in that guarded fashion to protect our ankle. Just as there is no wrong or right way to practice meditation, there is no correct or incorrect way to respond to your sensations of pain.

An important practice where we move our attention throughout our different body parts is called a body scan (see detailed below). Beginning at the top of your head and working your way down, and then back up again, the body scan is a mindfulness practice that you can use to work with pain within the body.

While performing the body scan, we are attentive to sensations within our body, but we don't try to evaluate them or change what we find.

The qualities needed with the body scan are focus, acceptance, and clarity. Be patient with yourself, because they do take some time to develop. Always remind yourself that body scans work for any kind of pain, regardless of the cause.

Example of a meditation for pain relief:

- Use calm, deep breathing. Breathe slowly both in and out. Take time to observe each breath. Breathe deep. Breathe slow. Breathe calmly.
- Use passive awareness. Become aware of everything, but one thing at a time. Single out one noise at a time. Take notice of each breath, and of your pain. Your goal is to observe it all without trying to effect change.
- Perform a body scan meditation.
    1. Sit or lie comfortably and close your eyes. Take note of what it feels like to be you in this moment.
    2. Take a few deep breaths and see how your breathing feels in your body.
    3. Return your breathing to normal.
    4. Begin at your feet, and investigate anything you feel. See if you notice anything like: tingling, warmth, coolness, tension, pressure, or heaviness, etc. Check out what you can feel and what you cannot. Does it change while you are in the middle of your observation? How does it change?

5. Let's move on from the focus on your feet and bring awareness to any sensations you might be experiencing in your legs. What do you notice?

6. After you address your legs, move your attention to your back and butt. Are you feeling any pressure or sensations?

7. Next, explore your stomach and chest areas. Can you feel your breath as it goes in and out? Do you feel your heart beating? Is it steady, or pounding?

8. Shift your attention now to your hands, arms, and shoulders. Is the air totally still, or can you feel the air upon your skin? As before, take note of any sensations.

9. Moving on, you will explore your neck, face, and head regions. Imagine taking notice of these parts of your body for the first time. Can you feel your teeth? What do your nose or cheekbones feel like?

10. Finish off your body scan meditation by taking note of the top of your head. And before you end your session, take a moment to notice your body as a whole lying there. With practice, you can expand this meditation and break it down by fingers, toes, ankles, calves, knees, etc.

11. You can always continue the body scan by moving back and forth from head to toe a couple of times.

- Use awareness and acceptance. Always be aware of your thoughts, but don't try to change them. Accept each thought, but then allow it to move on.

- Focus on your breathing. Observe each one of your breaths. Breathe deep. Breathe slow. Breathe calmly.
- Repeat a meaningful mantra. Choose a mantra that is important to you. For example: "I am safe. I am loved."
- Use awareness and acceptance.
- Use calm breathing.
- Stretch briefly. Take this time to stretch your muscles and open your eyes. Reflect on your meditation experience and write about it in your journal.

The best meditation methods that increase concentration are: mindfulness, counting the breath cycles, and the body scan. At the end of your session, you will probably feel calm and relaxed. Perhaps you will find your mood to be improved. Regardless, your pain should be less noticeable and easier to tolerate. Even though each of these steps may take as little as two minutes, feel free to spend as much time as you want on any steps.

In addition, or instead of the body scan, there are several types of meditation that help you focus, relax your mind, and channel your pain.

- Mindful meditation. One of the most popular types of meditation is mindful meditation, and this has been acknowledged to help manage anxiety, pain, and stress. In addition to being popular, mindfulness meditation is also the most studied type of meditation. You can practice this by yourself or with an instructor. Either choice is really just a personal preference.
- Visualization meditation. Many find that visualization meditation, or guided imagery, helps by giving you something positive to focus on while you meditate. The

ultimate goal is to calm you down, reduce pain, and reduce your stress.

- Breathwork meditation. This is a meditation practice that utilizes breathing exercises to make a change in your breathing pattern, helping you to relax your mind. Often, this is used in conjunction with mindfulness meditation to increase your focus.

Be patient, you will become more practiced given time and will find the correct meditation method that works best for you. As your skills improve, you will find yourself able to reduce your pain and have a better quality of life.

Meditation is totally free, unless you are choosing to work with an instructor, and a perfect choice to help you manage your pain. With it, you just may find many of those aches and pains a distant memory and you may be able to reduce your stock of pain relievers.

In addition to meditation, you may also look for help within tai chi or yoga, so that you are adding some low-impact movements to your meditation regime. It's time to regain control of your life and reduce that chronic pain that you have been dealing with.

Case Study: Judith

"The initiator of my chronic pain began when I was just a small child. I was born without any hip sockets, so most of my childhood was spent in body casts after enduring surgery after surgery. Even though the surgeries were deemed successful, I still had random bouts of pain throughout my back, hips, and joints and some severe headaches. Many of my days were so painful that I had to stay home from school, thus missing a lot

161

of my classes, and my grades suffered, as did my friendships. I was in danger of being held back a grade because of poor attendance and grades. I was frustrated and upset that my few friends that I had left would now be in different classes from me and that would impact my self-esteem because of having no friends. My parents ended up hiring a tutor to help me at home to catch up, but the pain persisted.

"I began to wonder what kind of life I was going to be able to have with all these constant interruptions to my high school years. Would I be able to attend college? Most likely not, because being away from home and dealing with my pain would be an insurmountable task. Could I expect to handle a job? With all my frequent days of pain, I was sure that no employer would want to deal with someone like me and I became more depressed and fearful of my life ahead.

"My tutor began to teach me a bit about guided meditation to help me focus on my schoolwork. I'm not sure that either of us expected the results we began to see. After several months, I began to notice that I had fewer days that were unbearable and even the days that were bad seemed to be less intense.

"I was able to not only graduate high school, but was able to attend the local community college, while having my tutor at my side through it all. She was a wonderful woman who helped me to get through those tough teen years and supported me through college. I ended up working from home as a copywriter, which enabled me to take the really bad days easy. Without her help and the guided meditations that she brought into my life, I am not sure where I would have ended up."

Case study: Kathryn

"My original injury occurred during a gymnastics event. I had a particularly nasty fall from the uneven bars and since then I have suffered immensely.

"I experienced pain when I sat, stood, or lay down and was unable to find a comfortable position to exist in. I tried every pain pill on the market, pain patches, acupuncture, corticosteroid shots, surgery, physical therapy, heat compresses, yoga, and anything else I or the doctors could think of. I began to physically fail and my loss of muscle tone and weakness was unbearable because I had always been active and physically fit.

"I felt that I was losing control over my life and was worried how my chronic pain would affect me going forward. I had been on track for a sports scholarship, but that dream was gone and I faced the full brunt of college tuition with little help from my parents.

"While waiting in the doctor's office one day, I struck up a conversation with another person who was a few years my senior but had a similar story revolving around chronic pain. She said that in addition to her regimen of heat, acupuncture, and some over-the-counter pain relievers, she had found that meditation had helped her reduce some of her discomfort.

"Hopeful, I contacted the studio that she had recommended and was able to sign up for a class starting up just after the holidays. I have to admit I was skeptical and for the first few months I didn't notice a difference, but little by little, my pain began to reduce. My meditation practices helped teach me how to react to my pain. I know that I had lost hope of having a life, but meditation has helped me regain a possibility for a happier future."

A Boost for Immunity

How can you tell if you have a compromised immune system?

Do you feel that you are frequently sick? Do you feel tired all the time? Maybe you have other symptoms lurking about, but you just can't figure out what is wrong. It could be that your immune system is stressed and weakened.

Did you just get a horrible cold after those big midterm exams? You have spent untold hours studying and staying up late just to study for important tests, but that long-term stress can undermine your immune system. Why? Because stress decreases your white blood cells, which help you fight off infections. This leaves you more at risk when exposed to viruses.

Are you always getting a cold or can't shake one off? While catching two colds each year is normal, they normally run their course in ten days or less. During the initial three to four days, your immune system kicks to develop antibodies to fight off your infection. However, if you find that you are catching constant colds or that they are lasting longer than average, it could be a sign that your immune system is struggling.

Another problem you face with a compromised immune system is you can experience a lot of digestive issues. If you have recurring instances of diarrhea, gas, or constipation, you may have low amounts of helpful gut bacteria. This can open you up to risks of viruses or autoimmune disorders. Up to seventy percent of your immune system is located in your digestive tract!

Have you ever experienced a cut, burn, or scrape that just takes forever to heal? Your immune system is what sends nutrient-rich blood to your injuries to assist in the regeneration of new skin. If your immune system is compromised, your skin will have difficulties regenerating and you will experience longer healing times.

Do you feel tired all the time? Often, this is just a sign of insufficient sleep, and as teens, this is a frequent problem because of school hours, homework, after-school jobs, and more. However, if you feel you are getting enough sleep and you are still suffering from fatigue, then your immune system may be struggling. When your immune system is stressed, your energy levels tend to plummet.

Within a given year do you feel that you have excessive bouts of infection? If you always seem to be struggling with constant ear infections, sinusitis, asthmatic bronchitis, or pneumonia, you will probably discover that your immune system is weakened.

If you find that your immune system kicks in too often, you may experience it beginning to attack your body instead of healing it. This may be a sign of a bigger underlying issue, like an autoimmune disorder. We encourage you to be proactive and while you are self-monitoring, be sure to enlighten your parents if you think you are experiencing troubling issues.

We have just learned how we can retrain our brains to help influence pain reduction, but did you know that we can also boost our immunity by similar methods?

Our autonomic nervous system, or ANS, is the part of our nervous system designed to control unconscious bodily functions such as breathing, pupil dilation, blood pressure, internal organs, our heartbeats, and our digestive processes. This system works within each of us automatically.

While these functions within us are technically on autopilot, our brains also use the ANS as a means of communication with our immune system. Researchers have recently become intrigued by the possibilities that mindfulness can have a positive impact on our immune system.

Our immune system is a fascinating protector against invaders. No, not alien invaders, but harmful invaders like viruses or bacteria. The first impression of our immune system was one of immune cells attacking invading cells on a physical level. In the 1980s, however, the immune system was reclassified after a series of studies found it to be extremely intelligent. As a result, it was often referred to as a floating brain.

The immune system has a precise recognition and detection protocol in place that can quickly distinguish between detrimental pathogens and our own healthy cells and tissue. It has the ability to communicate with the brain using chemical messages that travel within our bodies. If you find that your immune system is weakened, as a result of an autoimmune disease, chronic stress, or those pesky invading pathogens, your body will not operate normally. When our immune system is compromised, it leaves an open door for infection and disease.

Everything we experience negatively—stress, pain, low self-esteem, and depression—can directly impact our immune systems. Being compromised makes us susceptible. Stress can cover a lot of ground too, because we can get stressed from not eating right, being too busy, being in pain, not getting the proper rest, or being bogged down with homework. All these stresses lead up to vulnerability.

Mindfulness has proven to be impactful on the areas within our brains that act as our command center for immunity. When these areas are stimulated, they function more effectively. In this way, meditation has proven to be beneficial in reducing anxiety, depression, and helping to build immunity. And research is always being done in this area because we just don't have all the answers as to how. All we know for sure is that regular meditation greatly impacts and strengthens your body to help fight off dangerous infections.

Meditation is a basic essential that manages to alter our body's processes and boost our moods, in addition to enhancing the immune system's ability to fight infection. We are all standing at the forefront of meditation, rewriting our concept of biology due to all the changes scientists are studying.

The human body is composed of trillions of microorganisms, most of these reside in our "second brain," or our gut. What goes on in the gut helps develop and maintain our immune system. Since stress reduction can play an important part in maintaining a healthy immune system, it is only a natural conclusion that mindfulness would then affect our immune gut health by reducing our stress.

When you practice mindfulness meditation, you focus on the present moment and the natural response for your body is to calm down. This is what allows your immune system to do what it is supposed to do. Take care of you.

When practiced consistently, meditation and mindfulness enhance the immune system, but it can have an added bonus if you are struggling with an addiction. Since substance abuse can destroy your physical health, mindfulness can help restore it. When you incorporate meditations regularly, they aid in the healing of mind, body, and soul.

So what can you change about your routine to help boost your immunity?

- Commit to a regular meditation schedule that includes both morning and night.
- Reduce and avoid stress as much as possible.
- Make sure that you are getting adequate sleep.
- Practice mindful eating.
- Add some low-impact exercises like yoga or tai chi.

While you have listened to me go on about meditation and mindfulness, you may be thinking I am spreading a "too good to be true" claim. Remember that meditation takes a lot of practice and hard work to be effective. Meditation is not going to make dramatic changes overnight, but rather over time it can prove to be calming and effective when reaching for your goal of overall health.

Deep breathing through your meditation exercises helps you focus on what is occurring. The act of deep breathing is essential because it lowers the body's stress and makes you less prone to illness. We have researched some yoga breathing exercises to help you find your calm and boost your immunity. Please find them listed below:

- **Conqueror breath.** Also known as Ujjayi (oo-jy, meaning to conquer, or be victorious). This is a great place for a beginner to start because it quiets the brain while slowing your flow of breath. Conqueror breath is a foundation upon which many other techniques are designed, and it is recognized by the soft hissing sound that is produced by inhaling and exhaling over the back of the throat.
    - First, inhale through your nose. You will exhale through an open mouth, drawing the exhale breath across the back of your throat while producing a "HA" sound. After repeating this several times, close your mouth, and now inhale and exhale just through your nose, but direct the breath to still slowly travel across the back of

your throat. You should hear a slight hissing sound.

○ This sound is called ajapa mantra (as-jop-ah mahn-trah). The ajapa mantra helps to slow your breath down and focus awareness.

○ Begin with somewhere between 5 and 8 minutes initially, and you can gradually increase these sessions up to fifteen minutes. When you finish with any session, return to normal breathing and then lie down in Savasana (shah-vahs-uh-nah, corpse pose, see next).

- **Corpse pose.** This is often referred to as a final relaxation pose. This pose asks your body to release beyond the simple act of relaxation. Upon initial study, it may seem like an easy feat, but Savasana can be difficult to learn and practice effectively. You must be able to lie completely still but remain fully aware and unattached. When performed correctly, you will be able to release all mental chatter and permit your body to process all the information it has just been given. The idea is to continue to be aware throughout the length of time in the pose. Savasana is probably the most important pose that you will practice, because it renews the mind, body, and spirit. While you may find that Savasana can be used at the beginning of a session, it is mostly found at the end of your practices. This allows you to relax completely, releasing any tension you still may be holding onto.

You perform the corpse pose by lying on your back and refraining from any effort to hold your limbs in place. If you suffer from low back pain, you can use a rolled-up blanket under your knees to help make your position more comfortable. Do not attempt to hold your legs in place, thereby restricting your feet from falling open to either side. Your arms will rest beside your body, but not touching, with your palms facing upward. Resist the urge to force your hands to remain open and allow your fingers to curl in. Use your shoulder blades as support by tucking them under you. During this final pose, you will relax your entire body, including your face. Your breathing should be natural, without you trying to manipulate it in any way. When you are first starting out, try and maintain this pose for 5 minutes. As you improve, try lengthening it to ten minutes. When you release your Savasana pose, emerge slowly, beginning with deeper breaths. Wiggle your fingers and toes, then stretch your arm above your head, performing a full body stretch similar to the stretch you do first thing in the morning before getting out of bed. Bring your knees up to your chest, close your eyes, and roll over to one side. While in this position, you can use your bottom arm as a pillow while you rest in this position. When you are ready to bring yourself up into a sitting position, use your hands for support. It sounds relatively easy to do nothing for ten minutes, but in our fast-paced world, you may be surprised at how difficult it may be.

- **Single nostril breath.** This practice is also referred to as alternate nostril breathing. The practice of either Suya Bhedana or Chandra Bhedana centers around not only controlling your breathing, but breathing through one nostril while manually closing the other. There are two different versions of single nostril breathing. The practice of single nostril breathing has been proven to have a balancing effect between both hemispheres of the brain, and can reduce blood pressure.

○ Surya Bhedana (sun-piercing breath, soor-yah beh-dah-na). This version of single nostril breathing is thought to increase body heat and stimulate the brain.

The sun-piercing breath associates your right nostril with your body's heating energy, and the cooling energy of the moon is represented by the left nostril. It is believed that when your body is compromised, these energies are in conflict with each other. The purpose of the two breaths, whether surya bhedana or chandra bhedana, is to balance the breaths by warming a cool energy and vice versa. Sit in a comfortable position on the floor with your legs crossed and hands resting on your knees. Using either your right or left hand, gently close and block your left nostril while you inhale through your right. Then, you will close your right nostril while opening your left and exhale through your left nostril. Remember to begin slowly, perhaps performing this only a few times at first and then building up to around fifteen minutes.

○ Chandra Bhedana (moon-piercing breath, chahn-drah beh-dah-na). Since chandra bhedana is the opposite of surya bhedana, it is reasonable to assume that it cools the body and quiets the brain.

In order to perform the Chandra Bhedana, simply reverse the above process. It is advised that you do not practice these if you have high blood pressure or heart disease. And never do both breaths on the same day. Any questions should be directed toward your healthcare professional.

- **Mindful breathing.** This method can help you deal with the rollercoaster of ups and downs we experience. Mindful breathing assists in the calming quality of our breath. By being calm, we are less stressed, thus we do not tax our immune system. Practicing mindfulness makes us aware of what is happening in the moment and able to accept it at face value without trying to modify or control it. For those of you who may struggle with mindfulness, it is helpful to link the practice with breathing. If you can adjust your mindfulness practices, using breath as your starting point, it can open you to a whole new experience. Once you are able to breathe mindfully, you can call upon it at any time, at any place. It can work magically, like a genie granting a quick wish.

So right now, I imagine that you are very interested in this mindful breathing and want to know more about it, right? I promise that it sounds a lot more intimidating than it really is. Being mindful of your breath is just being aware of it without trying to control it in any way. Just breathe in, and breathe out. That's it! Simple, isn't it?

When you are first attempting to learn the ways of mindful breathing, it is recommended that you sit comfortably in a quiet place where you will remain undisturbed. With your eyes closed, focus on your breathing. Getting used to mindful breathing will not take you long. If you are able to practice it a couple of times a day for just a few minutes, you will be a champion in no time. Once you have become experienced in the practice of mindful breathing, you will find it to be your superpower that you can call upon at a moment's notice. Remember that in order to boost your immunity, you want to eliminate as much stress as possible in your life, so when you are feeling sad or worried, it might be time to don your superhero cape and flip the switch to mindful breathing. So, what have you got to lose? Let's try it right now.

Get comfy and close your eyes. Now take a mindful breath and feel the air enter through your nostrils, enter the body, and then back out your nose. As you breathe in and then out, experience the calm feelings with each action. Allow yourself to focus on the breath going in, and the breath going out. Merely notice your breath and don't try to control it in any way. Reach out and feel the peace this brings to you. While in this state, relinquish any issue you have bottled up inside you and let the problem drift away from you. If whatever was bothering you comes back into your mind, repeat the mindfulness breathing process until it no longer darkens your mind. This is the healing power you experience with mindfulness breathing.

- **Roaring lion, lion's breath, or simhasana.** This technique was discussed in Chapter 5.

According to a paper recently released by Ranch Creek Recovery (2020), a recent review that studied the effects of meditation and mindfulness on the immune system found a number of astonishing results. Meditation was found to:

- Increase the number of CD-4 cells, which are the cells that affect the immune system by sending signals to other cells, ordering them to destroy infection
- Reduce inflammation. The result of inflammation in a human system decreases immune function and opens the door for disease.
- Increase telomerase activity. Telomerase helps to promote the stability of chromosomes, preventing their deterioration.

This study has shown that through regular meditation, you can become healthier by strengthening your immune system.

Case study: Darious

"I was doing fine until that fateful day during my first year in high school. That was the day that my mother died in a car accident and my life turned upside down. The years following were turbulent and I was filled with grief and depression. If things weren't already bad enough, a little over a year later, my father remarried and absolute hatred filled my heart for my stepmother. I lashed out at her every chance I got and took every opportunity to run away from home, intermittently skip school, or hide out at friends' houses, choosing to come home during the day when they were both at work. One of my crowd suggested that I try some drugs to help me forget and not feel so sad and angry. I soon began to smoke weed regularly in a small thicket of woods behind the school.

"When I wasn't high, I was stressed and my gut ached. Instead of skipping school, I just dropped out. It was around this time that my parents figured out what was really going on and that I needed intervention. They ended up sending me to a teen residential rehab place that offered a high school program.

"I rebelled at first, because I considered myself the "cool kid" that didn't need intervention and most certainly didn't need this meditation trash. I was annoyed at first how fake they seemed, no one could be that positive and friendly. But, now in retrospect, I see that it was me that was fake. I was putting up this angry front to shut everyone out.

"My addiction had given me a false sense of security and I believed the angry negative voices in my head. I finally caved in and tried the meditation practices that they were offering to me. I was full of doubt regarding their claims of quieting the negative voices, boosting my immune system, and helping to ease my depression and anger. After the first day, I felt no different and my anger surged. I felt they had lied to me. The counselor assured me that it takes longer than one session and that I may not see much in the way of results for weeks. In addition, they explained that meditation was a lifestyle choice that would most likely travel with me through my lifetime.

"I won't lie. It was a long, hard road for me, but I started to see a change in the way I thought and how I felt. I watched the other teens around me gain success and return home. I became determined to do the same and completed the program, returned home and got back into school. I even found a part-time job at a local nursery. My job turned into full-time and I began to make plans to attend the local community college. I practice meditation every day because I found that it does help me deal with the pressures of balancing work and school. I find I am no longer angry, and my depression symptoms are lessened."

Chapter 7: Achieving Better Sleep

"When I'm worried and I can't sleep, I count my blessings instead of sheep and I fall asleep, counting my blessings." Irving Berlin, White Christmas

There probably isn't a teen out there who gets enough sleep! The problem is that sleep is essential at this time in your life because the teenage years are when your brain and body go through their most significant development. While you transition into an adult, these changes can affect family life, social life, and emotional development.

Teens need as much as ten hours of sleep per night. When you factor in school, homework, a possible after-school job, and chores at the home, it leaves time for little else. When they don't get proper rest, teens will tend to experience a lack of attention and a tiredness that may harm not only their school performance, but could endanger their health, even their lives.

Since sleep deprivation can affect the frontal lobe of the brain, which controls impulsive behavior, teens may find that they are making some poor choices without really understanding the reasoning behind it. Many questions regarding teen behavior in this regard come to the same conclusion that teens are lacking in sleep. Teens that do not get enough sleep tend to engage in activities with higher risk, such as drunk driving, texting while driving, drug and/or alcohol use, fighting, and carrying weapons. Vehicular accidents are more likely to occur because someone hasn't had enough sleep. This could result in being severely injured or injuring others all because of being sleepy.

The inability to get proper rest can result in a number of sleep disorders like insomnia, obstructive sleep apnea, and narcolepsy, but it can also impact long-term health.

"I can vividly remember how desperate I felt. Looking back, I am unable to pinpoint which meditation techniques worked for me or remember how long it took before I noticed a change. I was beginning my sophomore year and I was always so keyed up at bedtime that I only slept a few hours every night. I had turned into a zombie! I had been trying meditation for a few weeks and after the fourth week I began to see some results. I am glad that I stuck with it, and I have to admit I was tempted to give up a time or two. I had to really put in a lot of effort but now I am calm before bedtime and no longer need sleep aids. I continue to meditate every night before bedtime."–
Priscilla, 17

A good night's sleep is paramount to helping you regulate your hormones, power your immune system, and speed recovery to muscle and tissue injuries, but did you also know that a lack of sleep can have an impact on weight loss or gain? It's true! When we are unable to get the proper amount of rest, our bodies tell us that not only are we hungry, but we are craving high-fat, high-carbohydrate foods. So naturally, we head for the nearest junk food and caffeine to give us that quick sugar boost.

When we sleep less, we disrupt the thyroid, which produces less thyroid hormones, causing our metabolism to slow down. The food that we have consumed all day now has a higher chance of turning to fat and being stored in our tissues and organs, so if you are dieting, you will most likely experience a more difficult time dropping those few extra pounds.

In addition, sleep deprivation can be responsible for the development of some serious health issues, for example, high blood pressure, osteoporosis, muscle weakness, and mood swings.

Knowing now that sleep can have an impact upon us in both a negative and positive way, we should always make it a point to wind down every night, going from a busy, engaged mind to one that is calm. We have gathered a few tips to help you get the good night's sleep you need.

- Keep to a healthy sleeping schedule. Following a basic sleep schedule means that you will become sleepy around the same time each night and awake consistently around the same time each morning. This is the best and most effective way of getting the most out of your sleep. Keeping to this regulated schedule will allow you to wake up without too much trouble and you will find that your body becomes accustomed to regular cues. Not only will you be able to go to bed and get up around the same time each day, but you will also feel hungry on schedule. You will find that your mood will remain in the positive to neutral area and you are able to stay alert throughout the day. You have most likely experienced that a lack of sleep can cause frustration, moodiness, and aggression. Since we spend approximately one-third of our lives sleeping, we should attempt to get the best rest we can.
- It's hard to be in class the better part of the day, trying to be active. Let's face it, most days the only exercise you get is walking from one class to another. So if you take part in an after-school sport, it may be a great way to get your exercise daily. If team sports aren't for you, perhaps you could consider a short exercise routine for a short amount of time before you hit the books.

- Learn to wind down before bedtime. We get it, there are a lot of demands upon you right now, and you probably find yourself busy right up until bedtime. Then it happens—you try to go to sleep and you lie there feeling wide awake in bed! There's a simple solution, but it does take some effort to rework the bad habits that you have gotten into. Take an hour or two every night before bed and begin to prepare for sleep. Taking a warm shower or bath before bedtime is a good start. It takes time to prepare yourself for a good night's sleep and you need to engage only in things that produce low levels of excitement, such as reading (an actual book, not an electronic device), listening to calming music, or yoga and/or meditation.

- Never go to bed hungry or overfull. Always avoid eating a big meal before bedtime, because it will keep you up.

- Try not to nap. If you must nap, keep it limited and very short. Those long daytime naps will interfere with your quality of sleep at night and you may again find yourself unable to sleep or waking up during the night.

- Mindfulness meditation is where you pay attention to the present moment without judgment. The reason that this is helpful before a period of sleep is because it focuses on being. Your day has been supercharged and you have spent your day problem-solving and getting to class. While that is an important part of you, that is not the part that is going to help you catch some much needed z's. Mindfulness will take you from your "doing" self into your simple "being" self, and this is the one that is needed for a good night's rest. Sleep is not something you "do," sleep is a natural bodily need that you cannot resist. Sleep will always find a way to happen, but it would be really embarrassing if that moment was in American history class, wouldn't it?

- Minimize blue light and get rid of all those electronic gizmos. The release of blue light in the evening can block your natural release of melatonin, impeding your chances of receiving a good night's sleep. The earlier in the evening you put these devices away (preferably out of your room so you will not be tempted to cheat), the better.
- Learn to empty your brain at night. There was probably a lot going on at school today. Some may be challenges with schoolwork, but others may be social in nature. We tend to take the day's experiences to bed with us and we may toss and turn while we let them destroy our sleep. Instead, use your journal or a simple pen and paper to write down everything filling your brain. The ability to write down this kind of list will help you with thoughts that you are harboring deep inside of your psyche. Think of it as a free-flowing, random thought dump.

You can experiment with other calming activities as well:

- Reading a physical book or magazine (non-electronic)
- Audiobooks
- Calming music
- Crafting
- Painting or other art work
- Taking Fido for a walk
- Solitaire (using real cards, again, no electronics)
- Yoga, meditation, mindfulness

Give it some thought; can you come up with more?

How can you tell if your wind-down techniques are working? Are you able to fall asleep within a half hour of your desired time? If not, you should take a closer look at that targeted time before bed and assess where you are going wrong. You can begin by keeping track of your sleeping habits. For example, did you eat too close to bedtime? Did you ingest any caffeinated products during the late afternoon, like coffee, Coke, or chocolate? When you came home from school, did you take a nap? If so, how long was the nap? Did you spend too much time in bed without actually sleeping? When did you begin a wind-down before bedtime? During the wind-down time, did you give in to the temptation to check your social media or chat with a friend, even briefly? Any of these questions and more can throw you off your schedule of a targeted bedtime. Always track what time you get into bed and when you turn off the light to try and fall asleep. Keep track of times you woke up during your slumber and if they were lengthy breaks. Also keep a record of evenings that you used a calming activity and compare those evenings to ones that you do not use them. Do you see a difference? You may not even realize that you are interfering with your internal clock when you sneak a quick peek at your group's chat before bedtime. If you are worried that you might miss something important, take comfort in the fact that it will most likely be the same when you wake in the morning. We understand that making changes to your habits is never easy, but in order to be successful you must keep track of all those iced coffees and energy drinks that you consume.

Your inability to get a good night's sleep may also come from other problems you face. Do you feel overly stressed or depressed? These factors can influence your sleeping patterns.

Are you an early bird or a night owl?

Most teens will probably say that they are night owls and for very simple reasons. A teen's body waits longer to produce the naturally occurring melatonin (the hormone that promotes sleep), and this is why teens don't start to feel tired until later in the evening. Ideally, if teens were able to set their own sleep schedule, they would most likely go to sleep around midnight and wake around 9 a.m., but the problem with that is that darn school schedule. Since school starts early in the morning, teens have difficulties getting the proper amount of rest and end up with reduced sleep hours. Unfortunately, the majority of teens simply aren't able to get enough rest because of scheduling!

If you are one of the rare early birds, that means as long as you keep scheduled to wind down an hour before bedtime and can be asleep around 10 p.m., you should be able to get enough sleep. If however, you are an unlucky night owl, you will have to work harder to develop good sleep habits. Keeping the same sleep hours through the weekend will help set you up for a successful sleep habit.

Meditation for Sleep Disorders

So you have tried some of our tips for relaxing and getting a good night's sleep, but still you say you are experiencing difficulties.

There are some sleep disorders like insomnia and sleep apnea, which can cause breaks in your peaceful slumber. In this chapter, we will discuss some of these sleep disorders and meditation and mindfulness approaches to help you.

Insomnia

Insomnia is one of the more common sleep disorders that causes problems in your sleep habit. If you find it hard to fall or stay asleep, wake up several times throughout the night, or wake too early and cannot get back to sleep, this is a sign of insomnia. Were you aware that there are actually two different kinds of insomnia?

- Primary Insomnia is when your sleep difficulties aren't tied to any other health condition. This can be tied to life events such as an upsetting home life, moving, or loss of a family member. It can also be caused by bad sleeping habits.

- Secondary Insomnia means that you are suffering from a health condition that is causing you to have trouble sleeping. Examples could be depression, stress, or chronic pain.

In most cases, some lifestyle changes will help improve your quality of sleep when dealing with insomnia.

- If you start by keeping regular sleep hours, you can train your body to go to bed and get up regularly.

- Your bedroom should be an inviting, restful place. Temperature, noise, and lighting can all influence your sleeping environment.
- Make sure that your bed is comfortable because it is really tough to get a good night's sleep on a lumpy, too soft, too hard, or too small mattress.
- Cut out the caffeine! Try drinking warm milk or chamomile tea before bedtime.
- Spend time relaxing before bed. Listen to quiet, calming music, or do some gentle yoga.
- Practice mindfulness and guided meditations.

Yoga is an excellent choice for insomnia sufferers. It is gentle and restores your self. The key lies not in the poses alone, but with the breath that you use to perform them. The gentle calming breath technique for yoga is called ujjayi breath. To perform ujjayi breath with the exercises below (except the corpse pose where your breath should remain normal), inhale deeply through your nose, keeping your mouth closed. Now exhale through your nose but restrict your throat like you are saying "HA;" your mouth should remain closed.

When you practice yoga daily, studies show that you are able to sleep longer and fall asleep more quickly. You will find that adding yoga to your bedtime routine will help restore your sense of balance. It is important to practice the correct type of yoga to help you relax, such as hatha and nidra. Below, you can find several poses that will help you prepare for a good night's sleep.

- **Lying butterfly.** Lie on your floor on your back. Press the bottoms of your feet against each other, letting your knees fall out to the sides. (Using a pillow under your knees is okay, if this feels uncomfortable.)

- **Corpse pose.** Lie on the floor with your back straight and arms by your side with your palms facing up. Do not try and control your fingers or toes to hold a position, let them curl or point. Breathe slowly and pay attention to your breathing.
- **Legs against the wall.** Lie on the floor and put the back of your legs up against the wall, while keeping them straight. Your body should be in an L-shaped pose. Relax in this position for thirty seconds and focus on your breathing.
- **Standing forward bend.** Stand with your feet directly under your hips and inhale deeply. Exhale and extend your body forward and down, over your legs, to aid in the lengthening of your spine. You can either let your hands rest on your shins, the floor, or hold onto your elbows. The purpose of this is to relax, so do not try to force any part of the movement. If you have a back injury, you can place blocks under each of your hands for better support. Breathe in and out smoothly through your nose. You can also gently relax your head and neck muscles by using a yes and no motion. Stand slowly to avoid the sensation of lightheadedness. You can also modify this position to a standing half forward bend.
- **The wide-knee child's pose.** This is a resting pose that provides the practitioner with a sense of calm. Anyone having knee or hip injuries should sit this one out. Kneel on your floor, bringing your big toes together. Hold your knees hips-width apart, while you exhale and lay your body onto your thighs. Your hands should rest beside you, pointing to the back of the room with your palms facing up. Doing this should release any shoulder

tension. Your forehead should be on the ground and while in this position, gently roll your head from side to side. Breathe slowly and steadily.

- **Reclining bound angle.** This yoga pose eases any tension you may find in your hips. If you currently have a knee, hip, or groin injury, you may want to hold off on this one until you are over your injury. Lie down on the floor and as you bend your knees, place your feet on the floor. Continue by bringing the soles of your feet together, allowing your knees to relax and open away from each other. You can place pillows under your knees to help support your hips. Relax your arms on the floor at or about a forty-five degree angle from your body, with your palms up and facing the ceiling. Do not force your knees down, just allow them to be at a natural and comfortable position. You should experience a gentle but not painful sensation of stretching in your hips.

- **Legs on a chair pose.** This pose is for teens who may experience difficulties trying to extend their legs up a wall. Use a nice study chair and place a folded towel or blanket over the seat. When you lie down in front of the chair, get as close to the front of the chair as you can while in a fetal position. As you roll onto your back, keep your knees bent so that your calves will be resting on the seat of the chair. In this position, you should notice that your thighs will be at a ninety degree angle to your shins. Keep your arms relaxed at your sides, with your palms facing up. Remember to focus on your breathing.

- **Big toe pose.** This pose helps activate your parasympathetic nervous system, which is paramount in reducing tension within the body. To begin, stand with your feet apart and directly under your hips. After you gently bend forward from your hips, grip your big toes with your index finger, middle finger, and thumb of each hand respectively. Bend your elbows, and relax your head and neck. Breathe deeply, holding as long as you can up to three minutes.

- **Extended puppy pose.** This pose helps to counter the effects of sitting at desks during your long school day. The gentle forehead massage involved in this movement stimulates the pituitary gland, producing melatonin. To perform the extended puppy pose get down on all fours, while keeping your hips directly over your knees. Gently walk your hands and fingers forward until they come up over your head as you relax your chest and forehead down toward the floor. To massage your forehead, gently roll your forehead back and forth across the floor from left to right.

At the end of your yoga session, it can be very beneficial to end up with a body scan exercise (found in Chapter 6).

Need some yoga poses to get you going in the morning? If you have difficulties getting out of bed each morning, try the mountain pose, it will help you create some energy before starting your day.

- **The mountain pose.** This pose is performed by standing tall with your feet in alignment with your hips. Your arms are at your side. Inhale slowly and deeply while raising your arms toward the ceiling and keeping your palms facing each other. While you reach gently for the ceiling, slowly look up. After performing about five deep breaths, exhale slowly, and gently return your head and arms to their original position.

Having Problems With Your Sleep?

Periodic Limb Movement Disorder (PLMD) & Restless Leg Syndrome (RLS)

RLS is a common condition where someone has an irresistible urge to move their legs because of an uncomfortable sensation and can occur when either sitting up or lying down. This is referred to as a chronic medical issue that can last years or the duration of your lifetime. With restless leg syndrome, in addition to the constant urge to move your legs, you can also experience pain in the leg, difficulty falling asleep, fatigue, charley horses, tingling or burning, and sleep disturbances. Restless leg syndrome can start when you are any age and can be linked to an iron or vitamin D deficiency. It is advised that you obtain a blood test to rule this out. RLS is usually something that will be a lifetime struggle, so it is important for you to have ways of coping in place. Often some simple changes in your lifestyle can help with your symptoms. There is no known reason for the cause of restless leg syndrome, and women seem to be at a higher risk than men.

- Try baths and massages to help relax your muscles.
- Alternating hot and cold packs may lessen your sensations.
- Use excellent sleep hygiene for a cool, quiet, and comfortable sleeping area. Keep to a regular schedule of bedtime and wake up time, and make sure you are getting at least seven hours of sleep.
- Avoid caffeine.
- There is a foot wrap designed especially for people suffering from RLS. It is designed to put pressure under your foot.
- Get some exercise! It is preferable to keep your exercise low impact, and you are better off performing these earlier in the day. Working out too late may actually make your symptoms worse. Get your exercise sessions in at least 6 hours before bedtime.
- Mindful meditation and Yoga have both proven to give RLS sufferers some relief. Because it can be difficult to do the usual guided meditations with RLS, many sufferers have stated that a walking guided meditation works better for them. To begin a walking meditation, make sure that you pick a quiet place. Start with a slow and comfortable pace, and while you are walking, focus your attention on your breathing and your balance. Allow your mind to wander if it wants to. Your meditation walk can last around ten minutes to begin with. You can look into some pre-recorded meditations

that last anywhere from fifteen to forty-five minutes. The yoga poses for RLS are similar to the list above for insomnia. Refer to the above list for:

- o Legs against the wall
- o The standing forward bend or the seated forward fold. In the seated forward fold, you are just able to perform the standing forward bend by sitting on the floor.
- o Seated forward fold variation. While seated on the floor, you can alternate bending one knee and holding your foot in by your thigh. Remember to focus on your breathing.
- o The child's pose
- o The corpse pose
- o Use your deep breathing. At night, you can focus on your calm breathing. You can also practice the alternate nostril breathing.

Don't allow RLS to ruin your quality of life. Reducing your stress levels will help with your symptom severity.

PLMD is also a limb movement disorder, but is not the same thing as RLS. Periodic limb movement disorder can best be described as brief twitches, jerking movements, or experiencing your feet flexing upward. Movements can be in one or both legs and these actions can last a few minutes or several hours. Symptoms to look for are:

- Your knee, ankle, and big toe joints will all bend as part of the movements.
- You may experience anything from slight movement to wild thrashing and kicking.

Like RLS, the exact cause for PLMD is unknown. While some individuals can have both PLMD and RLS, subjects can have one without the other. Periodic limb movement disorder can cause daytime fatigue due to insomnia and has sometimes been linked to diabetes, Parkinson's disease, or anemia. Many teens experience poor sleep and don't connect the dots to issues with involuntary leg movements. Like RLS, there is no cure for these neurological issues, but the symptoms can be muted. The recommendations for PLMD and RLS in regards to guided meditation and yoga are virtually the same.

Obstructive Sleep Apnea

If you suffer from obstructive sleep apnea, you literally stop breathing for ten seconds or more many times throughout a night's sleep. When this action takes place, your brain and the rest of your body are deprived of oxygen. Possible sleep apnea characteristics may include:

- Loud snoring
- Sleepiness
- High blood pressure
- Someone actually observes you stop breathing while you sleep
- Gasping or choking
- Mouth breathing
- Teeth grinding or clenching

- Sweating at night
- Always tired
- Growth issues
- Morning headaches & daytime sleepiness
- Significantly overweight
- Being male

While this is typically more of an adult malady, teens can suffer from this sleep disorder and it can be dangerous if left untreated. Teens who suffer from hay fever may have a runny nose, congestion, or post-nasal drip, and when the nose is blocked, mouth breathing becomes more likely. Just because someone may snore, that does not mean that they have developed sleep apnea. This may contribute to the cause of sleep apnea and heavy snoring. There are breathing assistance devices available that can help keep airways open during sleep. A lot of people find these devices uncomfortable and are looking for more natural ways to combat sleep apnea.

Whatever your approach might be, sleep apnea can lead to some serious health issues, so it should always be addressed with your healthcare provider. The following can help you avoid sleep apnea:

- Maintain a healthy weight.
- Change your sleep position. Sleeping on your back can worsen the symptoms of sleep apnea. Shifting to sleeping on your side may help your breathing return to normal.
- Try using a humidifier or a diffuser. Dry air is known to irritate your air passages and using a humidifier will add moisture to the air. By doing this, you can help your airways open up and clear congestion. You can also use a diffuser with pure essential oils like lavender or

eucalyptus, which are dog-safe, but not for kitties!

- Meditation. In a recent clinical study, scientists from Keck Medicine of USC & UCLA studied a group of sleep apnea sufferers (2020) and found that using mindfulness meditation for a group of sleep apnea sufferers had better results for a good night's sleep than those who did not practice meditation. The meditation group reported a reduction in sleeping problems and a decrease in fatigue and depression during their daytime hours. Some common sleep meditations include:
  - Mindfulness meditation. When you practice mindfulness meditation, you focus completely on the present moment. Wandering minds will always happen, but the point of mindfulness meditation is to gently bring your mind back to right now. Coupled with breathing exercises, you will find that your body and mind relax. This can be achieved in as little as fifteen minutes each day.
  - Guided meditations. These are sessions that are either led by a teacher in a group, or you can find them online as audio recordings. A guided meditation is a popular choice with beginners because a lot of the work is already done for you. All you need to do is relax and listen as you are guided through your meditation. A type of guided meditation for you to look into is yoga nidra, which is also sometimes referred to as "yoga sleep." This particular meditation is said to help you reach the space between sleep and wakefulness. In reality, our bodies remain in this

state for only 3 to 5 minutes, but yoga nidra is designed to keep you in the wakefulness state for often forty-five minutes. If you build slowly, you should be able to attain yoga nidra.

○ Concentrative meditation. This meditation comes from Buddhist teachings and instructs you to concentrate totally on one thing. It can be a thought, an object, a mantra, or an image, for example a candle flame or a work of art. Using concentrative meditation calms both the mind and body and helps build patience and discipline.

• Yoga, of course! Yoga, through repetition, helps train the mind and body in positive ways. Yoga can help reduce the symptoms associated with sleep apnea because breathing exercises help strengthen airway muscles, and they reduce stress, giving you a better quality of sleep and the ability to live your life better.

○ **Breathing technique.** Use this yoga breathing technique. Begin by inhaling through your nose and exhaling slowly through your wide open mouth making the "HA" sound. After several repetitions of this process, close your mouth and continue to inhale and exhale through your nose, continuing to make the "HA" sound. When you begin, start slowly and build your time, but do not exceed fifteen minutes because this could cause a strain to the muscles within your throat. This particular exercise in breathing helps your throat muscles when you are a sleep apnea sufferer. You will notice that it helps regulate your breath, quiet your mind, and reduce stress.

- ○ **Cat-cow** (described in Chapter 5)
- ○ **The seated forward bend** (Chapter 5)
- ○ **Seated twist** (Chapter 5)

Idiopathic Hypersomnia

This chronic neurological disorder is when you feel the need to fall asleep during the day, even though you have had a full night's sleep. If you suffer from idiopathic hypersomnia, you will find that you sleep normal, or even a bit longer than normal, amounts of time each night, but you still feel overly sleepy. You may even take long naps, but end up often waking up worse than prior to the nap. Teens who suffer from this can find thinking clearly and basic physical tasks to be extremely difficult. Symptoms often first appear in the mid to late teens, although they can also begin earlier. If you are experiencing excessive daytime sleepiness for at least three months, you may have idiopathic hypersomnia. Currently, the cause for this disorder is not known. To minimize its severity:

- Stay hydrated.
- Avoid high-sugar and high-carbohydrate meals/snacks.
- Aromatherapy. Some recent studies have shown aromatherapy can help with your memory and cognitive skills. Peppermint oil and citrus oils have been the most commonly suggested to help you get through a test or task. These may improve your quality of life. Make sure that you are using pure oils with no added chemicals and

be aware that some oils are dangerous for pets. Always ask your healthcare provider and do your research.

- Mindfulness. Building your meditation skills can help with the symptoms of idiopathic hypersomnia. Try meditations, such as a walking meditation.
- Yoga. Many people with this condition tend to lead inactive lives, so taking the time to regularly stretch and flex your muscles with mini yoga workouts is a fantastic way to start and end your day. These workouts will take only about ten minutes each and can help you get that quick morning pick-me-up or assist you in winding down at the end of a stressful day.
  - Morning routine. Using these basic exercises will help get a jumpstart to your day. You can do these before you even get out of bed!
    - **Single leg stretch.** Lie on your back and bend your knees to your chest, keeping your toes pointed. Lift your head and shoulders up off the bed or floor. Relax the front of your neck and look at your knees. Inhale, and as you do this, draw your left knee toward your chest while extending your right leg about forty-five degrees above the bed/floor. Repeat using your opposite side and continue up to ten repetitions each side.
    - **Rolling like a ball.** You can either sit on your bed or floor for this movement. Bending your knees will move your spine into a C curve. Place your hands lightly on your knees, inhale, and rock back until

the bottom of your shoulder blades touches the bed/floor. Exhale and pull your navel to your spine pulling yourself back up into the original balance. Repeat up to ten times.

- **Windshield wiper.** Lie on your back and hold your knees bent at a ninety degree angle. Your arms should be extended out to your sides, while keeping your shoulders relaxed and having contact with the bed/floor. Inhale. Exhale, and drop both knees to one side. Inhale and lift your legs back to the original position. Exhale, and drop both knees to the opposite side. Repeat up to ten times.

- **Single leg circles.** Lie on the bed/floor with your right leg extended to the sky. (You can bend the knee ninety degrees if your hamstrings are tight.) Your left leg should be flat on the bed/floor. Now point your right foot and rotate the leg. Inhale. Now trace a small circle on the ceiling with your toe. To do this, move the entire leg from the hip socket. You can perform this up to ten times, then switch sides and perform another ten.

- **Half rollback.** Sit tall on your bed/floor with your knees bent. Your hands should be placed behind the thighs and feet. Inhale, roll halfway back (your spine should be rounded into a C curve). Hold for three breaths and then roll back up into a seated position. You can do this up to 5 times.

○ Evening routine. These can be done right after you get home from school or right before bedtime. These exercises will help you reduce tension and stress. You can play some quiet music or light some candles while you engage in this session aimed at stress relief.

■ **Warrior one.** Stand with your feet wide apart and lunge forward with your right front leg. While in this stance, you will be pointing your front toes straight ahead while turning your back toes in slightly. Keep your knee over the toes and your back leg straight. Your back foot should stay flat on the ground during this movement. Inhale and lift your arms overhead. While in your lunge pose, take 6 deep breaths. Repeat on the other side. You can do up to ten of these.

■ **Side plank.** Sit on the floor and hold your legs off to the right side. Place your left hand on the floor in line with your shoulder. At this point you can do one of two options. Either stack your feet, or keep the bottom knee on the floor as you lift your body. Extend your right arm toward the ceiling. Try to keep your body in one plane, and hold for several seconds, and then lower yourself back down. Repeat on the other side. You can do up to ten times each side.

- **Forward bend with chest expansion.** Interlace your fingers behind your back. (You can use a towel if your hands do not reach.) While bending at the hips, position your body into a forward bend. Drop your forehead toward your knees, and while doing this, stretch your arms in the direction of the ceiling. Hold for about twenty seconds. This can be done up to ten times.

- **Cat-cow stretch.** As previously described, begin on all fours with your knees tucked under your hips and your wrists directly under your shoulders. Exhale. Round your back up toward the ceiling, while dropping your head. Next, inhale and lift your head up, arching your back while extending your spine from your neck to your tailbone. Repeat this up to ten times.

- **Pigeon pose.** Begin this movement with your hands placed on the floor on either side of your right bent knee. Your left leg should be extended back behind you. Bring your right knee toward the right hand, turning your foot so that the top of your foot is facing the floor near your left hand. If you find this uncomfortable, you can move the foot back toward your groin. Sink into your hips, but keep them square to the floor. Walk your hands out in front of you in order to stretch the back and relax into the pose. Hold twenty seconds. Repeat using the opposite side. Repeat five times each side.

- **Legs up the wall.** Your last relaxation pose in this recommended group is legs up the wall. Lie with your back on the floor and your legs/feet up the wall or at the side of your bed with your legs at a ninety degree angle. Raise both legs in the air and straighten your knees as much as you can. While you relax, keep your arms at your sides and practice breathing deeply.

Narcolepsy

While narcolepsy can appear differently from person to person, it is typically described as a neurological disorder where REM sleep infringes into the realm of wakefulness. This is also a lifetime issue, but symptoms can improve a bit over time. All narcolepsy sufferers will have excessive daytime sleepiness, but only a small percentage will have to face all the other symptoms.

Symptoms include:

- Falling asleep during the day without meaning to, often at inappropriate moments.
- Cataplexy is a sudden loss of muscle strength that is often caused by a sudden strong emotion such as laughter, being frightened, or being angered. The loss of muscle control can have effects like a mild buckling of the legs or a complete collapse on the floor.
- Hallucinations can be experienced while falling asleep or waking up. Powerful and frightening images can occur with this sleep disorder.
- Sleep paralysis. This is described best as waking from sleep but being briefly unable to move. Sleep paralysis can also appear on its own without being tied to narcolepsy.
- Excessive daytime sleepiness. All narcolepsy sufferers will have EDS. No matter how much sleep a subject receives the night before, they will always be plagued by sleepiness. But unlike idiopathic hypersomnia, narcolepsy is like being attacked by an overwhelming sense of sleepiness or "sleep attack."
- Automatic behaviors. Teens with narcolepsy can experience momentary sleep episodes that can last mere seconds, but if in the middle of an activity—for example, a conversation—they can continue with the conversation and not be aware of what they are doing.

Since narcolepsy can vary, a person does not have to have all of these symptoms. As with all the sleep disorders we are presenting here, there is no cure for narcolepsy. However there are some lifestyle changes which can help the symptoms.

- Take short naps.
- Maintain a regular sleep schedule.
- Avoid caffeine. If you do have caffeine, make sure that it is several hours before bedtime.
- Don't use electronics before bedtime.
- Cut out sources of stress.
- Exercise every day. If you can exercise for at least twenty minutes each day and keep these sessions to at least five hours before bedtime, it may help improve sleep quality.
- Relax before bedtime.
- Mindfulness. Take time to surround yourself with positive messages. Meditation and mindfulness can help quiet the mind, making you feel more centered and in control. It may even assist with a better quality of sleep. The powerful meditation of Qigong can help improve your narcolepsy proclivities. Qigong, (pronounced chee-gong) is a part of ancient traditional Chinese medicine that combines physical movement, relaxation, and breathing exercises to either restore or maintain balance. Qigong is all about understanding and the strength of nature.
- Yoga. The practice of yoga provides benefits for mind, body, and soul, but can also help assist you with getting better sleep. Below, you will find many poses that we have already discussed and several more. Remember, as we mentioned before, these exercises should not be done right before you go to sleep, but preferably around five hours before bedtime.
  - **The standing forward bend** (earlier in this chapter)
  - **The cat-cow stretch** (Chapter 5)

- The child pose. This movement can help calm the nervous system and enhance your sleep. Begin this movement on your hands and knees. As you stretch forward with your arms, sit down on your heels. After extending your arms forward, you should be touching your forehead to the ground. Hold that position, and then inhale as you return to your original position.
- The butterfly pose. You begin this pose by sitting on the floor with your legs extended in front of you. Now, inhale and bring your feet toward you, making the soles touch each other. With gentle and slow motions, move your knees up and down so that you can experience the stretch in your groin area. Hold your breath the length of four or five breaths, exhale, and repeat.
- The spinal twist. Lie on your bed or floor, having your body form a T-shape. Fold your left knee and bring it gently up toward your chest. Your right leg should be kept relatively straight. Now turn your head and torso toward the left while bringing your left knee to the right. Hold for a few seconds, then gently return to your starting position and switch legs. You can also do this with both knees together as a variable in the exercise.
- The happy baby pose. While on your back, bring your knees toward your chest slightly spread apart, and while pushing your heels to the ceiling, grab your big toes with your fingers. In this position, you should be able to rock back and

forth slowly in order to massage the spine.
- ○ **The corpse pose** (Chapter 6)
- ○ **The nighttime goddess pose.** Lie on your back and bend your knees so that the soles of your feet touch. Allow your knees to fall naturally, and if needed for support, you can place a rolled up towel under your knees. Draw your arms up over your head with palms facing the ceiling. Hold for a few seconds.
- ○ **Legs up the wall pose** (earlier in this chapter)

Night Terrors

Most night terrors last somewhere around the ten-minute mark in length, but can last up to forty minutes and typically occur during the first several hours of sleep. An example of night terrors will have a subject suddenly show signs of panic and can include screaming, flailing, rapid heartbeat, dilation of pupils, and tensing of the muscles. While a teen experiencing a night terror may have their eyes open, they are not responsive to those trying to wake them during their distress. Subjects will rarely have any memory of the episode the following morning.

It is advised to not try and wake someone during a night terror unless they are in danger. Attempts to wake someone during a night terror could result in making the event last longer. While these events can be very frightening to the observer, the subject will usually fall back to sleep quickly.

Night terrors can be hit or miss because they don't occur nightly and do not keep to any schedule. Sufferers could have one a year or two per month. This malady can be triggered by stress, sleep deprivation, or by the onset of another sleep disorder.

While the cause of night terrors is not definitive, it can be genetic. While most of the sufferers of night terrors are young children, it can carry over into the teen years and adulthood.

Is a nightmare, a night terror? A nightmare can give someone a horrible fright and cause distress, but nightmares occur in REM sleep as opposed to the night terror, which takes place prior to REM sleep. It is more than likely that you will remember your nightmare in the morning, down to the last detail.

Below are some factors that have been recognized as triggering a night terror:

- Sleep deprivation
- Emotional distress or conflict
- A disruption in the sleep schedule
- Head injuries
- Some medications

Improving sleep quality is a typical approach for this, so make sure that you are getting enough sleep, keep to a sleep schedule, and make sure that the bedroom is cool and comfortable. Here are a few other tips to help curb night terrors.

- Don't eat or drink just before bed. Stick to water only.
- Avoid caffeine.
- Remove digital distractions at least two hours before bedtime.
- Try to get some daily exercise, but not before bedtime.
- Practice some relaxation techniques. This can include listening to music, reading (non-digital), or perhaps some yoga. (Many of the exercises used in the above sleep disorders will apply.)
- Guided meditation. A guided meditation may be just the remedy for someone experiencing night terrors. Luckily, there are many of them out there available on audio discs, etc. You can just relax and concentrate on your breathing while the recording does all the work. Guided meditations can take you to wondrous places where clouds can dance across the skies, birds will chirp melodiously, and you can eat marshmallow pies.

Sleepwalking

While most people outgrow sleepwalking, there is a small percentage of the population that continues to have difficulties into their teen and adult years. Sleepwalking is just like it sounds, the subject will get up and walk around while asleep. The typical time for a sleepwalker to have an occurrence is after one or two hours of falling asleep. A sleepwalking episode usually lasts only a few minutes, but there are exceptions that may last longer. The characteristics that define a sleepwalker are:

- Rising from bed and moving around
- Sitting up in bed with the subject's eyes wide open and having an unusual, glazed expression on their face
- Does not respond to others
- Not remembering the episode in the morning
- May perform routine things like getting dressed, or eating
- May leave the house
- Talking in their sleep
- May exhibit unusual behavior
- May try to drive a car!

Sleepwalking is not a huge cause for concern; what the subject can do while sleepwalking is another matter. They can and often do hurt themselves by walking into furniture, falling down stairs, wandering about outside, or as above, trying to drive a car. Even though you may be tempted, you should never wake a sleepwalker. The reactions to being awakened may prove injurious for both of you, they may just reach out and hit you.

Just gently guide them back to bed and make soft calming statements. Ways to curb the sleepwalking include:

- Keeping to a sleep schedule
- Keeping the bedroom cool and dark. Make sure that your mattress is comfy!
- Get rid of the electronics at least 2 hours before bedtime.
- Limit caffeine intake.
- Get some exercise during the day.
- Diffusing lavender, vetiver, or clary sage may help with slumber. Make sure you are using pure essential oils and check carefully for any danger to house pets.
- Try a nice decaffeinated tea like chamomile.
- Guided meditations

Since sleepwalking can be the result of not enough sleep or too much stress, it is natural to look at some guided meditations for someone who has trouble in this area.

Exercises for Mindful Sleep

If you are looking to improve the quality of your sleep, then mindfulness exercises and techniques can help change your habits to achieve healthy sleep cycles. Everyone has a minute to spare so let's start there!

One-Minute Meditation

This mindfulness exercise helps us reset our breath, creating a deeper awareness in the present moment. This simple technique will let your body know that you are ready for a rest. This can be used right when you snuggle under the covers for bedtime or at any point, day or night, when you feel the need to reset.

Take a few moments to scan your body, finding what part of you wants to let go and relax a little. Take a full, deep breath in, filling your lungs and expanding your chest. Then breathe out slowly, feeling all the sensations as you release. Now repeat those two breaths again, before allowing yourself to return to your normal way of breathing. Open your senses and feel your breath in the foreground while relaxing the sensations found in the background.

Insomnia Can Be a Real Struggle

Whether you have trouble falling asleep or staying asleep, you still wake with the feeling of inadequate rest and this can affect people of all ages and backgrounds. There are meditation music pieces that specifically target the insomniac. You can find this music that targets your Seven Chakras free on YouTube® by using the seven solfeggio frequencies (a score for the teaching of sight-singing whereby the score is sung to a special syllable; in English-speaking countries you may recognize these as do, re, mi fa, sol, la, ti).

It can be hard to explain why a tired person goes to bed at a reasonable hour only to wake up a few hours later feeling like it's time to get up. By using meditation music you should be able to fall asleep faster and remain in a deeper slumber for longer periods.

Releasing your worry before sleep can help you achieve that deep slumber you have been looking for. Let go of your worries before falling into a peaceful sleep, and don't pressure yourself into forcing a certain outcome. Your peaceful state should come naturally when combined with soothing music to help you achieve your deep slumber. You should awaken refreshed and carefree.

Take in a deep breath, breathing in through your nose, then release gradually. Now take another, feeling your diaphragm expand, then exhale, and notice how your body feels. Take notice of how you feel, and take time to connect to your body. Return your breathing to your natural rhythm and you should notice that you feel heavier.

Not only will this exercise help you achieve a deeper sleep, but you will feel a relief from the aches, pains, and feelings of stress that you carry around with you. Never force any change and realize that each of us is both perfect and needs calmness to help us change. Be in the moment, but don't worry about perfection. Enjoy each breath as you are drawn deeper and deeper into relaxation. Allow all your thoughts surrounding your day to fade, and replace them with a calming sensation. Allow your thoughts to float by, leaving you in a feeling of gentle peace. Let any worries that surface fade away, allowing you to be free from concerns and feel refreshed.

Focus on your breathing in your natural rhythm. Picture a garden and graceful butterflies that flutter from flower to flower, enjoying the garden that you have provided for them. Their graceful movements allow you to breathe slower and deeper as they continue their ballet from blossom to blossom. In the background, you can hear the gentle flutter of a hummingbird's wings and the soft buzz of a bumblebee hard at work pollinating the buds in your garden. Across the meadow, you hear the gentle coo of a morning dove calling for its mate.

You have found a safe place to rest, away from your daily stresses. Let your body slumber.

Surrender Meditation

As you prepare for sleep, surrender to the love and wisdom that embraces all of us. When you surrender before you sleep, release all your worries and fears that keep you from enjoying the peaceful rest you require.

Using breath awareness and your body scan technique, you can let go of your need to retain complete control and surround yourself with the wonders of the universe.

Schedule Yourself a Time to Worry

This may sound like it goes against everything we have been saying, but if you make time to worry and release, then you will not take it to bed with you like a disheveled teddy bear. By using this exercise, you can gain a new perspective on any worrying thoughts you may have and still gain a deeper sense of awareness.

The best time to set aside your worry time is 15 to 30 minutes during the morning or afternoon. That keeps it far away from your bedtime. By practicing this, you can develop control over your worries, keeping them to designated periods and freeing up your other time to enjoy the world around you. Try these steps to help you schedule a worry window.

1. Schedule a worry time each day for the period of a week and mark it in your calendar. Set aside 15 minutes during the morning or afternoon as your designated worry time. Never schedule a worry time before bedtime.

2. During your 15 minutes, take time to write down any worries you think of. You should not pressure yourself to solve anything during this window unless your mind naturally goes there. The writing alone of these worrisome thoughts can prove to be therapeutic and can often give us perspective when we see it written in black and white.

3. Always remind yourself that only the 15-minute block is set aside for worry time and worries outside of this time are not allowed.

4. If you find your thoughts drifting back toward worry outside of your designated time, tell yourself firmly that those thoughts are not allowed until the next worry period. It will be difficult to become used to this new habit, but try restricting your worries to only the designated worry time. Given practice, your intention and effort will pay off and make a difference.

5. At the end of each week, take a few minutes to reflect upon what you wrote down during the week. Do you notice any telltale patterns or repeat worries? If you find that you have recurring worries that appear over and over again, don't worry because that is a very common occurrence.

6. After trying this method for a week, try it for another, and as you gain practice, you will begin to notice an ability to control when you are allowed to worry.

I've had a lot of worries in my life, most of which never happened.

— Mark Twain, author and humorist

Mindfulness Activity: Breathing With Your Mind

- Place the tip of your tongue against the ridge behind your upper set of teeth. You will be keeping it there throughout this activity.
- Exhale all your air through your mouth. You should hear a whooshing sound.
- After your exhalation, close your mouth. Now inhale through your nose, counting to four.

- Hold your breath for 7 counts.
- Again, exhale slowly from your mouth as you count to eight. You should still be making the whooshing sound.
- Repeat this cycle four times.

Activity: Keep A Sleep Diary

You will need some paper and a ruler and pen. You will want eight columns across and several rows down depending upon how many questions you choose to use for your chart. We have provided a sample of the first row for you below.

Question column	Day 1	Day 2	Day 3	Day 4	Day 5	Day 6	Day 7

Under the question column fill in with examples like you find below, or make up some of your own.

- Did I take a nap today? If so, how long was this nap?
- Did I exercise today?
- Did I meditate today? When and for how long?
- Record what time you go to bed each night.
- How much time did you dedicate to winding down each night before bedtime?
- How long before bedtime did you cease the use of all electronic devices, for example phones, tablets, computers?
- Did you have any caffeine products within four hours of bedtime?
- After getting into bed, how long did it take you to fall asleep?

- Was my sleep disturbed because of: a cold, allergies, noise, pets, or pain?
- After falling asleep, did you wake up during the night? If so, how many times?
- If you add all these sleep interruptions together, how long in total were you awake during the night?
- What time did you wake up/alarm went off?
- How many times did you hit the snooze button?
- What time did you get out of bed?
- What was the length of time you spent in bed from the time you initially got into bed until the time you got out of bed?
- On a scale of one to ten, with one being poor and ten being excellent, how would you rate the quality of your sleep?

Activities to Help You Achieve Inner Peace

Everyone suffers from those anxiety-filled days. Here are a few ways to find a quick calm:

- Close your eyes. By closing your eyes you can effectively shut off the sensory information that your eyes feed to your brain. Even just a few moments can give you the break you need from whatever stimulation is affecting you. You may be surprised at how calm you feel after just a few moments!
- Breathe like a dragon. In other words, be fierce. While sitting or kneeling, inhale deeply through your nose, then exhale through your mouth. As an option when you exhale, stick out your tongue! Focusing on your breathing always helps to break up the tension.

- Apply pressure. An acupressure key point can be found between your thumb and index finger. If you want to alleviate some pain or a panic attack, try this area or one of the others. You can also apply pressure between your eyebrows or on your inner forearm just above your wrist.
- Make your bed. It's such a simple thing to do, but you may be surprised at what tucking in your sheets and fluffing your pillows can do for you and your mental state. This can be the cornerstone of how you kick off your day and build upon your good habits, producing a happier you.
- Pen a gratitude list. A quick list of things and people you are grateful for can help overcome your stress.

- Take a chocolate break! Everyone's favorite thing to do is indulge, but chocolate is all about those flavanols found in dark chocolate. These act as antioxidants and can also benefit your brain function by increasing blood flow. Just don't overdo it, and only indulge in moderation.

Chapter 8: Meditations – Writing Your Own

Right now you have probably gotten inspired as you've read through the materials here, and you may be excited about the thought of creating your own meditations. After you have some meditation miles under your belt, it is only natural that you want to try creating your own with your writing abilities. By penning your own meditations, you can personalize your experiences and enjoy content directed at your favorite places or pastimes, whether real or imagined. For example, you may choose to write one based upon a favorite vacation to the Grand Canyon, meditating on the beach, or cruising on a bicycle.

Every person uses both hemispheres of the brain, but usually the right or left is more developed than the other. An interesting thing about the activity of writing is that the writer uses both the left and right hemispheres of the brain. This act all by itself can slow the process of aging and give you unique insights on how to connect with your subconscious. Since people tend to not have many neural connections between the right and left brain, when we use them to write, it makes us smarter.

So how do you get started? Begin by setting the right intention. For example, you want to move to a new state. The reason you want to go is not because you hate your life or you're tired and want a new start. You want to move to this place because you love yourself and you believe you will be happy in this new place.

Meditation and the writing of your own personalized journey is powerful. When you do this action, you usually are able to see what blocks you because you are connecting with your subconscious. Our blocks often remain hidden to us because we spend much of our time on autopilot.

Set Your Intention

Let's start by setting your intention. The main idea here is to speak to your subconscious and give it instructions. This can be achievable by relaxing as if you are going to meditate, and the visualization can help you determine more easily what it is you want to write about. Here is an example of setting intention:

"Attention Universe, I am ready. Let's begin my quest. I know that this will take me many places and I realize that I need to release my worries. I am ready to understand the reasons behind them and I am ready to act accordingly to improve them. I trust in your guidance and know that I am cared for and loved. I choose not to worry anymore. I am ready to take my deep breaths and pick my solutions."

Repeat it every day; your subconscious will love it.

Observe Your Thoughts

Make yourself comfortable, take a deep breath, and close your eyes. Continue to breathe deeply and try to observe your thoughts. Don't panic, we will walk you through it.

With a bit of effort you will be well on your way to becoming a visual person. After all, every day that you look into a mirror, you see yourself staring back. Right now, imagine that you are looking at yourself in a mirror. Picture standing by your own side and observing how you sit and breathe deeply, all with your eyes closed, and you are peaceful. Write what you see.

This can be very confusing at first because we are not wired to observe ourselves consciously. What we want to stress here is that, unconsciously, people do this all the time! You stop to check your hair, your lipstick, or make sure that nothing from lunch is in between your teeth.

Connect With Your Subconsciousness

All of us possess an inner critic. Often it's one that chatters in our ear and whispers that we aren't worthy. When we are coping with stress, anxiety, depression, and pain, we find it difficult to silence this voice. You may have to dig deep to find out what belief is holding you back. When you are able to find that belief, this is what you want to change within yourself. When we write, we are able to open doors to our subconsciousness and let our amazing talents and gifts out to play.

Write every morning. You can detail what's on your mind, any pain or happiness you may be feeling, or what you may be angry, upset, or excited about. Imagine emerging from the depths of Mordor, to find a land free from worries and fear. Never lose sight that the ability to write is to be a genius.

Create Inspiration

Indulge your inner child and have some fun. Whether you want to visit a museum, go skating, or build a snowman, give yourself the gift of freedom. When you are able to do this, you may find some wonderful things lurking inside of you that have been dying to see the light of day.

Your inner child brings energy and joy for you and the people around you. Anytime that we need to calm down or remove worries, we can reflect on our inner child and all the freedom and happiness it brings.

Imagine

"Imagine all the people, living for today ..." – John Lennon, singer, songwriter

You are having a calm and relaxing day. Imagine saving that energy inside of you. When you have a sudden need to meditate or write your own meditation, you can reach inside of yourself and find your support.

The General Structure of a Guided Meditation

- Get comfortable. Just take a little time to prepare for your meditation and get comfortable. It doesn't matter if you are sitting or lying down. Inhale deeply through your nose using your diaphragm, then exhale all the air out through your mouth. Allow your mind to recognize anything negative that it may have had exposure to today and let it go. Reassure yourself that it's okay to let it go. Within this space, you are safe. You can begin to relax, because it is safe here. This time has been set aside just for you, and there is nowhere else you need to be, except right here.

- Start with a relaxation. Spend five to ten minutes describing the relaxation of the body and the mind. Use visualizations and/or breathing techniques. You can even incorporate a countdown if that appeals to you. In order to help yourself relax, you can script something like: relax your toes, relax your legs, relax your body, hands, arms, shoulders, neck, head and forehead, (you get the idea).

- The next step is writing your script so that you can begin your journey. You want to be kind and say nice things. For example, I am smart, I make great decisions, I am worthy of good things, or each step takes me where I want to be at this moment. Describe the environment that you want to experience. Remember to include all five senses—what is seen, smelled, heard, tasted, or touched/texture. The more involved you can become with the described place, the more deeply you will feel the connection. Take care to not drag the description out. Your imagination will fill in any missing blanks for you. Your guided meditation is going to help you reprogram your beliefs deep within your subconscious.

- The return. During your meditation, you will naturally respond by becoming very relaxed. The return to your normal everyday world should be done gently and gradually. For new writers, one of the easiest ways to return is to bring you back to your starting point.

- Once you have your script written out just the way you want it, you can record it. We recommend that you practice it several times so you are familiar with everything you wrote down. You can use your smartphone to record it, just like you would record a memo. Make sure you are satisfied with your recording and save it.

Success! You have just made your first personalized guided meditation. After all that hard work, make sure that you listen to it every day to experience real change.

Guided Meditation Example #1

- Sit or lie down, whichever is more comfortable to you. Close your eyes and take notice of your breathing. Is it quick, or slow and steady?
- Take a deep breath from your diaphragm in through your nose and out through your mouth. Notice the air coming into your lungs and take note of how that feels. Now make the same observations as you exhale. Breathe like this a few more times before we begin our journey.
- You have nothing to worry about, you are safe, and nothing can hurt you. We arrive at a stable where we are going for a nice trail ride. You are assigned a nice, safe horse to ride and put your left foot in the left stirrup. You swing up with ease and put your right foot into the right stirrup. Take another long breath.
- Your horse begins to follow the others and as you leave the stable, you can feel a gentle summer breeze across

your face. You can smell the horse with his comforting earthy scent along with the smell of the leather saddle you sit on astride his broad back. Your horse snorts, and you can feel the reverberation throughout his rib cage directly beneath your legs.

- As you ride through the forest at the base of a large hill, you can smell the dew upon the grass and the blossoms in the trees. Throughout the field you can see many wildflowers mixing in with the tall grasses and you can smell how fragrant they are as their scents drifts through the air. You can feel the steady four-beat stride of your horse's walk. It is comforting to you.

- Out from under the tree cover you see a path winding up the hill. You are all on this path. You close your eyes for a moment and soak in the gentle warmth of the sun upon your face. As you open your eyes, you see wildlife all around you. Birds fly overhead and the rustling you heard behind you takes the form of a gentle doe and her fawn as they break out of the forest at a run. You and your mount stay calm and forge ahead.

- You have reached the top of the large hill, and you can see for miles all around. From here, you can almost imagine what it would be like to stand at the top of a huge mountain. Behind you lies the small forest you traveled through, and ahead of you is a downward trail that leads to a small beach.

- You and your horse travel down this trail and you can feel the power in his hindquarters as he shifts his weight to his backend to make his way down the hill, keeping both your bodies balanced.

- You can almost visualize being a rider from the old

west and how it might have felt to ride out into the open wilderness.

- The chirping of birds gently calls to you and you smile and look for them as they sail out across the water.
- You and your steed have finally reached the beach and you both take off at a nice, powerful canter through the edge of the water. As you breathe, you can feel each powerful rhythmic stride of your horse and the gentle splash of water droplets flying up to spray you with its warmth. The wind blows through your hair and you smile because you are happy.
- You stop and while standing still, you can see the sun reflected in the water and realize that it is time to return.
- Back up the hill and down into the forest you ride at an easy pace because you can feel that your horse has become a bit tired. That's okay. A nice, relaxing ride back to the stable is how you want to spend your time.
- Removing your right foot from its stirrup, you swing your leg up over the horse's back and lay across the saddle, kicking your other leg free and dropping to the ground beside your mount. You can feel the solid earth beneath your feet.
- You draw near the barn, and one of the stable hands takes your horse from you after you have dismounted.
- While you watch your horse walk away from you, he becomes smaller and smaller. Gently, you open your eyes and you are home.

Guided Meditation Example #2

- Sit or lie down, whichever is more comfortable to you. Close your eyes and take notice of your breathing. Is it quick, or slow and steady?
- Take a deep breath from your diaphragm—in through your nose and out through your mouth. Notice the air coming into your lungs and take note of how that feels. Now make the same observation as you exhale. Breathe like this a few more times before we begin our journey.
- You have nothing to worry about, you are safe, and nothing can hurt you. You are sitting on a cushion outside in the grass. All around you are the smells of nature. With your next deep breath you can detect the sweet smell of lilacs permeating the air along with the smell of newly mowed grass.
- Feathered friends from nature are calling and you can hear the soft chirp of baby robins in a nearby nest.
- The neighbor's little dog barks and you can hear the excitement in his woofs as you picture him chasing a chipmunk, rabbit, or squirrel across his yard. Even though there is a high stockade fence between you both, you can hear his small feet as they hit the ground, running in the same direction as the rustling sounds of the wildlife he pursues.
- You can hear the melodic buzzing of honeybees as they fly from flower to flower, pollinating both floral and vegetable buds. A cloud passes over the sun and you can smell the oncoming rain in the air. Small droplets

fall in a scattered pattern.

- A gentle shower begins and you can feel small droplets of rain hitting you. When you look beneath the raspberry buds, you can see two young bumblebees hiding together to keep out of the rain. Nature is a magical place. There is something about nature that can put a smile on anyone's face.
- The shower ends and the sun emerges from behind a cloud. Noiseless wings carry butterflies into the garden, searching out water and pollen.
- In this moment you feel at peace. The nature that surrounds you provides you with harmony and instills calm.
- The time has come to rejoin the world. You have enjoyed your moments in the sun. Gently, you open your eyes, and you are home.

"I took a walk in the woods and came out taller than the trees." Henry David Thoreau, naturalist, essayist, and philosopher

Conclusion

I know that you have had a great deal of curiosity about mindful meditation and its impact on stress, anxiety, coping with depression, ADHD, chronic pain, and better sleep. So often there is misinformation out there surrounding meditation, and I hope that I have given you a sense of security so you can be at ease with your journey into mindful meditation.

The research that you are following is similar to any investigation that you might do into any passion. It's never easy to start something new, but the rewards will be worth the journey. Core meditation principles are easy and straightforward. The information and tips I have provided will enable you to succeed. Remember that:

- You may fail some days, but everyone does. You will persevere. I believe in you!
- You can recover drained energy and motivation by the methods of mindfulness and meditation. It's time to become invigorated and enlightened. Begin today!
- Never stress over getting started with meditating consistently. Start small and keep going. Stay focused.
- Meditation will lift your spirits in a way that you have never before experienced. Get ready to feel more peaceful, motivated, and positive!
- You will become changed and your new outlook will help you find better solutions to old problems. Armed with these new philosophies you will be able to clear your mind of anything negative and blossom.

Don't be discouraged if you don't find instant relief when you begin meditating. Please give your new habits a chance to work because the art of meditation is, in itself, its own language. There's no way you would be able to learn a second language in a week and meditation is no different. Because there are several different ways to meditate, it will take time to figure out which methods work best for you. We are confident that you will find which techniques work best for you.

I know that many teens out there are struggling with finding themselves during this time and the positive influence of mindfulness meditation will take you from ordinary to extraordinary. By following mantras and positive thinking, you will find the hidden artist within.

Meditation is a relatively inexpensive practice. There are a couple of apps out there that we recommended in our book that are free to use. Besides a yoga mat, there is little cost involved unless you attend a class for yoga or meditation. Mostly, you spend your time and effort and you receive so much more in return.

There is never a wrong way to practice mindfulness, and it's never too late to begin. Mindfulness meditation is a journey that will take time for you to achieve, but with patience, you will become successful and enjoy your freedom from stress, anxiety, and more. You will feel your energy improve and your self-esteem grow. And while you may never fully rid yourself completely of a disorder, you will be able to circumvent many of the symptoms.

I have touched briefly on meditation and mindfulness and provided you with different ways to meditate, the origin of meditation, and how to be successful by starting small and building up your sessions. In our other book: *Mindful Meditation for Teens & Pre-Teens: A Practical Guide with Examples, Meditations, and Tips To Reduce Stress, Improve Focus, Build Confidence and Self-Esteem, Improve Social Skills and Sleep Quality,* we cover a bit more ground on the basics. The beauty is that no path you choose will lead you astray, because meditation can be personalized for the practitioner.

In addition to case studies, we have included extra anecdotes from students who, like yourself, began their journey into meditation. You may notice that not all of them embraced this practice at first, but given time and results, slowly found what they desired. These are real teens, known to the author, with real problems, who have found their way despite some dark days.

You are on the path to becoming an adult, and with that maturing, you will be faced with new challenges that previous generations have not really experienced. Your gift and your curse is one born from the digital world. These devices have taken over the majority of our free time and many teens no longer have face-to-face communications. If you want to develop the skills necessary to conduct that interview and attain your dream job, then you will have to put away the phone.

We have provided many tips and suggestions in regards to activities, use of planners, and healthy alternatives to the way you think and eat. We have given several breathing activities and yoga exercises to help you develop your best defense against emotions that may plague you. In addition, we have encouraged you to experience nature, reading, writing, dancing, and music. It makes no difference which choices you make, because none of them are wrong.

The last thing we want is for you to feel frustrated at any time while on your journey. That is why we have encouraged you to never push for results, but to let them form naturally. This journey you have begun will last longer than any day, week, month, or year because this adventure will last you a lifetime.

I empathize with you as you are coping with signs of stress, anxiety, depression, chronic pain, and ADHD. Our latest worldwide test has been to deal with stay-at-home orders and the added stress that a global pandemic has added to our population.

Throughout the text, I have taken the time to detail the various health issues that can plague teens like you, and I have offered you insightful advice on how to cope with these issues and hopefully minimize your symptoms. I know that some of you have experienced some dark moments, but I pray that with mindfulness, the sun will shine on you again and inspire you to find what ignites your passion, so that you can take control of your destiny.

Finally, I challenge you to commit and start right away, even if you haven't finished reading all my tips, stories, and strategies. Begin simply, practicing your breath meditations for 5 minutes each day for a week and then start increasing either in increments or adding an evening meditation. If you find it challenging to commit to that much time, continue on with your shorter sessions. Consistency is the key to developing any habit. Increase when you can until you are able to meditate 20 minutes each day. You will watch your benefits unfold and bestow upon you great things.

A Guide Activities, Exercises, Tips and Case Studies

Throughout the book, you have found many activities and exercises that will help you start, continue and strengthen your mindfulness and meditation practice. You have also read meditations, healthy habit and mindset tips, as well as case studies of other teens who have found mindfulness and meditation helpful in many challenging situations.

You can refer to these exercises and tips and use them whenever you need them. To help you easily find the activities in the book, please use the handy reference guide below.

Activities

Mindfulness activities. (Page 13)

Activity 1: Spreadsheet for Your Feelings (Page 54)

Activity 2: Feeling Anxious? (Page 55)

Activity 3: Control Your Anxiety (Page 56)

Break out your journal (Page 75)

Activities to manage anxiety (Page 72)

Self-Compassion worksheets (Page 87)

Mindful steps to help depression (Page 97)

Body scan meditation (Page 114)

Meditation for pain relief (Page 158)

Breathing with your mind (Page 215)

Keep a sleep diary (Page 216)

Exercises

Focus on breathing. (Page 27)

Guided Meditation Example #1 (Page 224)

Guided Meditation Example #2 (Page 227)

Exercise 1: The Dolphin (Page 42)

Exercise 2: Self-Esteem (Page 43)

Emotional Awareness (Page 70)

Examples of journaling ideas (76)

Don't forget about doodling (Page 77)

It only takes 10 minutes (Page 95)

Do you run on autopilot test (Page 100)

Account for emotional avoidance (Page 101)

Draw a picture of depression (Page 102)

Breath awareness meditation (Page 103)

Building your focus through aromatics (108)

Exercise 1: STOP visualization exercise (Page 118)

Exercise 2: Study at home (Page 134)

Study at home exercises (Page 134)

Be silly (Page 137)

One minute meditation (Page 210)

Breathing with your mind (Page 215)

Keep a sleep diary (Page 216)

Activities to help you achieve inner peace (Page 217)

The general structure of a guided meditation (Page 222)

Tips

Success through meditation. (Page 9)

Getting started with meditation. (Page 31)

Nip Negativity (Page 73)

Watch those words (Page 74)

Using positive affirmations (Page 104)

Change your mindset (Page 106)

Boost your immunity (Page 168)

Impact your sleep (Page 185)

Insomnia can be a real struggle (Page 211)

Surrender meditation (Page 213)

Schedule yourself a time to worry (Page 214)

Set your intention (Page 220)

Observe your thoughts (Page 220)

Connect with your subconsciousness (Page 221)

Create inspiration (Page 221)

Case Studies

Terri (Page 39)

Ashley (Page 44)

Iris (Page 69)

Abagail (Page 119)

Kevin (Page 133)

Judith (Page 161)

Kathryn (Page 162)

Darious (Page 175)

About the Author:

Dana is a full-time working professional and parent of teens and young adults. They all dwell in a humble home that provides a magical backyard full of visiting squirrels, hungry rabbits, and fragrant skunks. The family breaks out their binoculars to enjoy the large variety of birds that visit their multiple bird feeders and then excitedly discuss any new bird that calls upon them.

Though familiar with meditation, Dana practiced only infrequently, and like many others, used a busy lifestyle as an excuse to put meditation off. Then her youngest teen was diagnosed with hyperactivity and ADHD in the beginning of high school. He was already worried about trying to fit in at his new school and then, on top of everything else, he was concerned about his diagnosis and how it might affect his schoolwork. He wondered "why me?".

A medical professional that was involved in his initial diagnosis suggested mindfulness meditation as a way to improve his focus and concentration. Dana's son found the meditation helpful in quieting his mind and boosting his concentration. Some of his stories are incorporated in this book and the previous title by the same author, *Mindful Meditation for Teens & Pre-Teens: A Practical Guide with Examples, Meditations, and Tips To Reduce Stress, Improve Focus, Build Confidence and Self-Esteem, Improve Social Skills and Sleep Quality*.

His journey inspired Dana to reach out with needed help for all the other teens in this world that wrestle with similar issues. This became the birth of this book and the prequel. If these teachings and the sharing of information that Dana has provided helps even a handful of teens, it will all have been worth it!

No matter what taunts you in your life, meditation can provide a better path to walk, and what seemed almost impossible to face before will be easier to handle and provide you with confidence.

"The goal of meditation isn't to control our thoughts, it's to stop letting them control you." – Anonymous

One Last Thing

I really hope you enjoyed this book. Would you mind taking a few seconds to leave a brief review of the book? It will help future readers like yourself, and it will help me as an author for a very long time.  THANK YOU

Leave a Review on Amazon:

References

Abblett, M. and Willard, C. (2016). *Mindfulness for teen depression : a workbook for improving your mood.* Oakland, Ca: Instant Help Books, An Imprint Of New Harbinger Publications, Inc.

Abdallah, C. G. and Geha, P. (2017). Chronic Pain and Chronic Stress: Two Sides of the Same Coin? *Chronic Stress*, 1, p.247054701770476.

Burdick, D. E. (2017). *Mindfulness for teens with ADHD : a skill-building workbook to help you focus & succeed.* Oakland, Ca: Instant Help, Books, An Imprint Of New Harbinger Publications, Inc.

Carney, C.E. (2020). *Goodnight mind for teens : skills to help you quiet noisy thoughts & get the sleep you need.* Oakland, Ca: Instant Help Books, An Imprint Of New Harbinger Publications, Inc.

CHADD. (2020). *Yoga for ADHD? Studies Show It Can Be Helpful.* [online] Available at: http://chadd.org/adhd-weekly/yoga-for-adhd-studies-show-it-can-be-helpful/ [Accessed 25 Jan. 2021].

The health benefits of tai chi. (2009). [online] Harvard Health. Available at: http://www.health.harvard.edu/staying-healthy/the-health-benefits-of-tai-chi/ [Accessed 25 Jan. 2021].

Higgins, J. (2010). *Energy Beverages: Content and Safety.* [online] National Center for Biotechnology Information. Available at: http://ncbi.nlm.nih.gov.pmc/articles/PMC2966367/ [Accessed 17 Jan. 2021].

Honos-Webb, L. (2010). *The ADHD workbook for teens : activities to help you gain motivation and confidence.* Oakland, Ca: Instant Help Books.

Kulman, R. (2020). *How to "Outgrow" ADHD with Motivation and Meditation.* [online] Psychology Today. Available at: https://www.psychologytoday.com/us/blog/screen-play/202011/how-outgrow-adhd-motivation-and-meditation [Accessed 4 Mar. 2021].

Medlineplus.gov. (2017). *Caffeine.* [online] Available at: https://medlineplus.gov/caffeine.html [Accessed 4 Mar. 2021].

Nelson, P. (2018). *There's a hole in my sidewalk : the romance of self-discovery.* New York: Atria Paperbacks.

NIMH» The Teen Brain: 7 Things to Know. (2020). [online] Available at: http://www.nimh.nih.gov/health/publications/the-teen-brain-7-things-to-know/index.shtml [Accessed 25 Jan. 2021].

9 Substance-Induced Disorders. (2005). [online] *www.ncbi.nlm.nih.gov.* Substance Abuse and Mental Health Services Administration (US). Available at: http://www.ncbi.nlm.nih.gov/books/NBK64178/ [Accessed 17 Jan. 2021].

Parekh, R. (2017). *psychiatry.org.* [online] www.psychiatry.org. Available at: http://www.psychiatry.org/patients-families/adha/what-is-adhd [Accessed 25 Jan. 2021].

Penman, D. (2015). *Can Mindfulness Meditation Really Reduce Pain and Suffering?* [online] Psychology Today. Available at: http://www.psychologytoday.com/us/blog/mindfulne ss-in-frantic-world/201501/can-mindfulness-meditation-really-reduce-pain-and-suffering/ [Accessed 26 Jan. 2021].

Poncelet, B. (2020). *Facts, Symptoms, and Causes of Teen Depression.* [online] Verywell Mind. Available at: http://www.verywellmind.com/teen-depression-3200844 [Accessed 25 Jan. 2021].

Porterfield, J. (2014). *Teen stress and anxiety.* New York: Rosen Publishing.

Press Trust of India (2018). *Stay calm and meditate, mindfulness can boost pain tolerance.* [online] Hindustan Times. Available at: http://www.hindustantimes.com/fitness/stay-calm-and-meditate-mindfulness-can-boost-pain-tolerance/story-mCW3dXQgiZEEMbi6kSv1AK.html [Accessed 11 Jan. 2021].

Raja, S. & Ashrafi, J. (2018). *PTSD SURVIVAL GUIDE FOR TEENS : strategies to overcome trauma, build resilience, and take ... back your life.* New Harbinger Publications.

Rissman, R. & Moutarde. (2017). *Yoga for you.* Lake Forest, Ca: Walter Foster Jr.

Schab, L. M. (2021). *The anxiety workbook for teens : activities to help you deal with anxiety and worry.* Oakland: New Harbinger Publications.

Schenk, S. (2016). *Yoga for teens*. Editorial: Twin Lakes, Wisconsin: Lotus Press.

Tompkins, M. A. (2020). *RELAXATION AND STRESS REDUCTION WORKBOOK FOR TEENS : cbt skills to help you deal with worry and ... anxiety*. New Harbinger Publications.

Transcendental Meditation Practice Alleviating ADHD in Caribbean Schools. (2013). [online] Transcendental Meditation (TM) For Women. Available at: https://tm-women.org/news-article-adhd/# [Accessed 4 Mar. 2021].

Image References

Aurelius, M. (2020). *Woman leaning on her table*. https://www.pexels.com/photo/woman-leaning-on-her-table-4064174/

Fairytale, E. (2020). *Woman practicing yoga*. https://www.pexels.com/photo/woman-practicing-yoga-3822631/

Natalie. (2019). *Photo of woman meditating.* https://www.pexels.com/photo/photo-of-woman-meditating-3759657/

Piacquadio, A. (2018). *Young troubled woman using laptop at home.* https://www.pexels.com/photo/young-troubled-woman-using-laptop-at-home-3755755/

Piacquadio, A. (2020). *Group of athletes practicing meditation in modern studio.* https://www.pexels.com/photo/group-of-athletes-practicing-meditation-in-modern-studio-4376968/

Pixabay. (2016). *Silhouette of tree near body of water during golden hour.* https://www.pexels.com/photo/silhouette-of-tree-near-body-of-water-during-golden-hour-36717/

Pixabay. (2019). https://www.pexels.com/photo/yoga-2959214/

Rodnae productions. (2020). *A girl covering her ears in front of her parents.* https://www.pexels.com/photo/a-girl-covering-her-ears-in-front-of-her-parents-6003570/

Shvets, A. (2020). *Woman with hands on her face in front of a laptop.*

https://www.pexels.com/photo/woman-with-hands-on-her-face-in-front-of-a-laptop-4226215/

Venter, M. (2016). *Photo of man sitting on a cave.* https://www.pexels.com/photo/photo-of-man-sitting-on-a-cave-1659437/

Made in the USA
Las Vegas, NV
19 January 2023

65917746R00144